ROMANCING YOUR CHILD'S HEART

MONTE SWAN

with Dr. David Biebel

VISION & STRATEGY

MANUAL

Multnomah® Publishers *Sisters, Oregon*

ROMANCING YOUR CHILD'S HEART: VISION AND STRATEGY MANUAL
published by Multnomah Publishers, Inc.
© 2003 by Monte Swan and David Biebel

International Standard Book Number: 1-59052-270-2

Published in connection with Loyal Arts Literary Agency, LoyalArts.com

Cover image by Getty Images/EyeWire Collection
Interior design by Katherine Lloyd, The DESK, Bend, Oregon

Unless otherwise indicated, Scripture quotations are from:
The Holy Bible, New King James Version
© 1984 by Thomas Nelson, Inc.

Other Scripture quotations are from:
The Holy Bible, New International Version (NIV)
© 1973, 1984 by International Bible Society,
used by permission of Zondervan Publishing House

Multnomah is a trademark of Multnomah Publishers, Inc.,
and is registered in the U.S. Patent and Trademark Office.
The colophon is a trademark of Multnomah Publishers, Inc.

Printed in the United States of America

For information:
MULTNOMAH PUBLISHERS, INC.
POST OFFICE BOX 1720
SISTERS, OREGON 97759

03 04 05 06 07 08—10 9 8 7 6 5 4 3 2 1 0

To the members of the first Romancing Your Child's Heart
parenting class at Lookout Mountain Community Church (LMCC),
who contributed a treasure trove of experience, insight, and
wisdom to this manual, and encouragement to us:
Jeanie & Bob Chase, John & Sheri Engstrom, Eric Gemelli,
Julie & Ernie Gilbert, Pablo Hadzeriga, Linda Hendrickson,
Larry & Mindy Howes, Jerry Isler, Donna Karns,
Toni & Jeff Olson, Randy Olsson,
Mary Rader, Mark & Holly Steller.
And to Karey Swan.

CONTENTS

FOREWORD

While I was working on this manual I called my cousin, Bekki, a wise mother of seven children. During the conversation I asked her what she felt was the primary need of parents today. "Communication," she replied. When I asked her to elaborate, she said, "Most fathers and mothers have not taken time to discuss their parenting approach…and fewer yet have developed a strategy of their own."

When Bekki said "of their own," she reinforced my conviction that the direction we had taken with this manual would help meet a major need of parents today. Even if ideas and concepts are sound, most people will tend not to follow through as decisively as they would had they come up with the ideas and concepts themselves. So the title *Romancing Your Child's Heart: Vision and Strategy Manual* acknowledges this basic tendency and strength of human nature.

I have written this companion to the book *Romancing Your Child's Heart* not to advise but to assist you in creating your own personal parenting approach, based on a renewed vision of what "biblical romancing" is all about. This manual is intended to coach, not to counsel. I had the pleasure of battle-testing it with a wonderful fellowship of parents from our church. During the last session, one of the mothers said that this experience had clarified her "parenting vision." She went on to say that the words of the ancient Irish hymn "Be Thou My Vision" poetically express that *the vision is God.* This interesting and insightful twist of words brings vision into the realm of relationship and away from formula.

You will also notice that I did not call this book a "study guide" or "workbook." Meeting the challenge of winning a heart is not about academic information, following a formula, or filling in the blanks. It is about embracing a vision and crafting a strategy—a game plan for the contest. You are in a relentless competition with a formidable suitor for the heart of your child. Your offense is your best defense against this powerful competitor. Although God's grace is the ultimate determining factor in the outcome, you must do as you would in any competition—establish your goals, strategize, train, prepare, learn how to wield the tools of romance skillfully and effectively. And then, of course, you must get in the game—you must show up for the contest.

Just as every child and parent is unique, so your strategy for each individual child will be unique, too. Knowing the battlefronts, the lay of the cultural landscape, the key heart issues, and the other suitor's tactics are all important. But the real issue is your own integrity—you must be credible, authentic Christians and persuasive, genuine parents.

(Sometimes the situation itself—for example, single parenting—will also affect your strategy, but this is a separate issue and is discussed in chapter 7.)

However, you must have been wooed to God to be able to woo your child. Who you are (in contrast to what or how much you know) is central to the romance because, at its core, romance is about relationship. So, the primary message that this manual will help you implement is not so much *propositional* (though its foundations are biblically, psychologically, and socially sound) as *relational*. Your child is more likely to choose God and His way of wisdom if his or her heart has been effectively romanced by you.

Admittedly, some of this terminology will seem new. But I am confident that those who move beyond the terminology to the reality of heart-to-heart communication, even communion, with their child, will have found a "pearl of great price" or a "treasure hidden in the field…[which] for joy over it...[a man] sells all that he has and buys that field" (see Matthew 13:44–46).

For though some of this terminology may be new in some ways, the story it reflects—the Larger Story, the kingdom story, the story of Jesus—is older than time itself. God, the original Romancer and the Hero of the story, woos hearts to Himself. His passionate love pulsates through the pages of both Old and New Testaments—the greatest romance ever written.

All of creation flows from the triune fellowship of God—all of life, all of history. We are created with the potential to share this perfect intimacy and relationship, and God has placed within each human heart a longing for it…an innate knowledge that we were made for something more. The central, underlying principle of the universe is not about survival, chaos, or chance, but about intimate relationship with our Creator, who loves us more than words can say and has been wooing us to Himself since before the beginning of time.

When this divine romance of our hearts becomes real for us, when its passion penetrates past our minds to our souls and we allow it to move us within, then we are ready to romance our children's hearts to this same loving God. Then the process will not be difficult, for its underlying currents will flow from our inner selves, like streams of refreshing, life-changing water, to everyone with whom we have relationship, including our children.

The goal of this manual is to help you craft the romance by developing and implementing a strategy to win your child's heart for Christ. The last few pages of the manual have been set aside for recording your thoughts and insights (journaling), learning, and growing, perhaps in the context of a group of your fellow parenting pilgrims. At the very end, you'll find a suggested outline to guide you in articulating your personal strategy to win your child's heart.

Beyond that, the implementation will be up to you. I wish you well and pray that your efforts will be fruitful—awakening in your child a heartfelt love for God and a genuine appreciation of His Story, of which our individual stories are single sentences. More, I pray a similar awakening for you, as your own sense of wonder, wisdom, and worship are rekindled once again through the process of learning, but especially through the experiences you and your child will share.

—Monte Swan, with David Biebel
March 2003

HOW TO USE
THIS MANUAL

A basic assumption of this manual is that those who use it will have read its companion book, *Romancing Your Child's Heart*. A second assumption is that, although the manual certainly can be used by individuals and couples, it will most often be used in a group setting.

Whatever the setting, you are encouraged to be creative, innovative, and flexible with the ideas offered. You should not feel obligated to answer every question or do every exercise. In most of the sessions, more suggestions are provided than can normally be dealt with in an hour or even ninety minutes. Use whatever is most pertinent to yourself or your group.

In each session you'll find questions for reflection or discussion, or suggested activities aimed at helping you personalize, internalize, and practice the basic concepts that are dealt with in the corresponding portion of the book. Sometimes short excerpts from the book are included, to be read out loud or silently as a way of refreshing and reinforcing its message.

We have included a "commencement" chapter at the very end, with discussion questions and exercises designed to further enhance your "covenant" to love your children in a new way. It is recommended that this be done as a day-long retreat.

If you work through this manual as a group, you'll need a leader. The leader's role in facilitating group activities is crucial. He or she must be responsible to coordinate details and anticipate the needs of the group for each session. The leader should also feel free to personalize the sessions with original stories, object lessons, film clips, music, and other aids.

Group Leader: Extremely important note for session 1. Using the instructions provided at the end of that session, construct the "arch" prior to the session and bring it to all subsequent sessions.

Where more discussion questions or activities are suggested than the group will have time to complete, the leader should prayerfully consider which of these would work best. However, the leader should remain open to the desires of group members to pursue a particular "unselected" direction from time to time.

The leader should try to keep things moving, while remaining sensitive to participants' needs to share as a part of growth, always keeping in mind not how much of a particular session's material has been covered but how much is happening in the hearts of the people involved. For the group, like the book, should be focused more on who people are and who they are becoming in Christ than on the facts they have memorized.

Toward the end of the entire process, if the group is meeting within the typical parameters of the quarterly schedule observed by many churches, one issue that will need to be settled will be whether—and if so, how—the group will use the "commencement" exercise at the end. Although this exercise, like most, can be completed by one couple, or perhaps several, it will have its greatest impact if as many as possible of the group's regular members can participate.

Some groups find it helpful to have an unofficial "contract" among themselves that outlines all or most of the issues below:

◎ The reason the group exists.
◎ The group's specific goals.
◎ How often, where, at what time, and for how long the group will meet per session.
◎ How long the group will exist.
◎ That participants will try to attend as often as possible (and will notify the group leader for a particular session if they will be late or absent).
◎ That members are willing to be held accountable for goals they set for themselves.

You may wish to discuss or review these at the beginning of your first meeting, exchanging other important information with each other, including name(s), telephone numbers, and so forth.

Finally, we suggest that the following basic group "rules" will enhance your time together:

1. No one should be forced to share. Not all questions apply to all people; not all people wish to share publicly on every subject. This is okay.

2. Personal matters that are shared in the group setting will be considered confidential and will not be shared outside the group without the speaker's permission.

3. No one should dominate the conversation. Everyone is there for the same purpose—to learn and to grow. Sometimes this happens through hearing what others say, sometimes through dialogue, sometimes through silent reflection, and sometimes through journaling.

4. Communication between participants should focus primarily on encouragement and never on judgment.

5. Arguments between participants, especially spouses, should not be allowed to last more than a couple of minutes. We'd put a smiley face on this one if we could, since we know that there will be differences of opinion as you discuss some of the questions we've proposed. Don't allow your "need to be right" to distract you from progressing toward your real goal.

Who are you to judge another's servant? To his own master he stands or falls. Indeed, he will be made to stand, for God is able to make him stand.
(Romans 14:4)

Part One

THE VISION

INTRODUCTION
TO PART ONE

T he primary purpose of part one of the manual (sessions 1–6) is to introduce romance as the core idea in the biblical parenting model. From this understanding a vision for using this idea can be constructed. "Vision" implies a special discernment, awareness, and sense of seeing—a single-mindedness. Our vision as Christian parents must be supernatural and should be focused on winning our child's heart for God. But it is also relational, for it is rooted in our personal relationship with Christ.

The love found in the Trinity, written about in the Song of Songs, personified by Jesus Christ, and offered on Calvary, is romantic. Romance is implied, required, and designed into the Gospel Story. It draws, woos, and ravishes the heart. Without it there would be no spiritual war; God would have crushed Satan. But God allows the war to be waged because of love. The battleground is the soul of man, and the prize of the romance is his heart.

Session 1, "Winning Your Child's Heart," shows that for a Christian, the highest goal can only be winning your child's heart. Session 2, "Remembering How God Won Your Heart," explores the participant's own stories of being romanced to God. Session 3, "Living in the Larger Story," challenges participants with a vision for the Larger Story, of which all our life stories are a part. Session 4, "Wooing Your Child with Story," shows that story is the language of the heart. Session 5, "Competition for Your Child's Heart," exposes Satan's strategy to win your child's heart. Session 6, "Watershed Choices," provides an overview of the whole romance.

Group Leader: Because part one (sessions 1–6) builds a theological foundation for the application of romance to parenting, it naturally lends itself to a lecture format. But this manual has been designed to stimulate sharing and creative thought, so you are encouraged to bring everyone into the discussions. The deeply personal nature of the parent/child relationship lends itself to emotional, heartfelt participation that will be of great value to all.

WINNING YOUR CHILD'S HEART

Life's only worth living if you've been loved by a kid.
—BUZZ LIGHTYEAR, *TOY STORY*

H e was a distinguished man dressed in a business suit. He sat rigidly next to his wife, just a few rows from the front. It was clear that he did not want to be there. As the hall filled, I nearly lost track of him in the crowd. As I began my presentation I saw him again and nearly lost track of my thoughts.

He was visibly shaken as I sang some words from a song I had never finished writing:

If you knew you had one year,
Left to live, left to love,
Would you live to love?
What would you do if you knew?

After the talk, entitled "Winning Your Child's Heart—Parenting's Highest Objective," I never saw the fellow leave, but his wife waited until the hall was almost empty, then walked up to me. I saw in her eyes an odd mixture of intense joy mingled with deep sorrow.

"I nearly had to drag my husband here," she began. "When I saw your title, I knew it was for us. We've already raised two kids—with one more still at home—a teenager. From all outward appearances the older ones are doing great—one's a lawyer and the other is finishing medical school—just like their father wanted. But something's missing. Until today I didn't know what it was. But now I do. We lost their hearts."

"Tell me what you mean," I replied.

"Well," she said, "it's like we're strangers now. We almost never hear from them, and

◎ Have someone read this aloud.

13

when we do all they talk about is their careers, the money they hope to make, the things they hope to buy—houses, cars, places they want to go…things like that. I had hoped we would be best friends, and that they would care about the things we care about, especially the things of God. But they don't. It's almost as if they've been bewitched…by materialism, or the world, or whatever…just like you talked about."

Her answer hung in the air as I wondered how she could be so sad and so happy at the same time.

Reflection/Discussion

1. Create a list of typical goals that parents have for their children. Which are legitimate goals for Christian parents?

2. Based on what you know so far about the couple in this story, what parenting goals had they embraced with their two older children?

3. What do you think is the source of this mother's pain?

◎ Continue reading aloud.

"You've described something very sad," I said, "and very difficult. Yet you're smiling. Why?"

"I was always afraid this might happen," she said. "But I trusted Roger—that's my husband's name. He's a businessman, and when he gets focused on a goal, nothing deters him. His goal was to equip our children with all the necessary tools, skills, knowledge, and experience so they would be successful in life. He structured career tracks for them, from honor classes to prestigious schools and finally toward brilliant careers."

"What parent wouldn't have that goal? What was there to be afraid of?"

"I couldn't name it until today," she said. "I just knew in my heart that in our rush toward success we were neglecting something very important. When you sang that song, Roger looked at me with tears in his eyes, and I knew that he finally understood. He whispered to me right then—I could hardly believe my ears: 'With Johnny (that's our youngest) we're going to do things differently,' he said. 'Whatever else happens, we have to try to win his heart.'"

Reflection/Discussion

1. What do you think Roger and his wife had been neglecting?

2. If you are a parent, have you ever felt that in your rush to raise your child, something was missing?

3. With Johnny, Roger wants to do things differently. What do you think he means?

4. If you were Roger, how would you begin?

List everything you can think of now. As you read the book and listen to others, this list will grow.

LEADER'S PRAYER: *Father, thank You for our children. We love them and want the best for them. For most of us, parenting will be the most challenging and most important mission in life. We realize that our children are treasures—gifts—arrows in our quivers. Make us a true community, comrades standing shoulder to shoulder as we enter the competition for our children's hearts. We pray that the romance of Christ will win their hearts for You. We acknowledge that we cannot do this through our own strength. We need each other, but most of all we need You. We ask that You would bring us together through Your Spirit, show us Your truth, and teach us to apply it to our parenting.*
   In the name of Jesus Christ our Savior and Lord, amen.

SESSION GOAL: **To help participants affirm that parenting's highest goal is winning their child's heart for God.**

SESSION OBJECTIVES

1. To view parenting from an eternal perspective.

2. To see romance as the keystone to reaching the goal.

For the LORD does not see as man sees; for man looks at the outward appearance, but the Lord looks at the heart. (1 Samuel 16:7)

Objective 1: To view parenting from an eternal perspective.

Roger (the father in the story) was a good and honorable man trying to give his children the best, but he had overlooked their hearts. He had it backwards—he had tried to gain the world for them and assumed that in the process he would automatically gain their hearts. He had protected his children from failure through excellent training, discipline, skill development, and knowledge attainment. From a temporal perspective he had done everything right.

But the simple words of an unfinished song cut through all that and forced him to view it from another perspective: "If you knew you had one year left to live, left to love…would you live to love? What would you do if you knew?"

Let's face it. Most parents—including most Christian parents—are a lot like Roger. Even before the children are born we talk about them, discuss how many we want and how we will raise them. We dream dreams, buy books, and pray prayers. We design our houses, select our vehicles, and even choose our careers with them in mind.

After their birth we spend thousands of dollars and thousands of hours educating and mentoring them, driving them to music lessons and athletic events. We buy swing sets, build tree houses, and order truckloads of sand. We provide musical instruments, computers, and sports equipment.

But what remains when they drive away one day? Are we left with a garage full of tennis shoes, old blue jeans, car seats, rocks, broken toys, and baseball gloves? Or have we built relationships, deep and strong, that will only get better over time?

We can do, do, and do until the cows come home, and still end up estranged from our children.

Reflection/Discussion

1. How is it possible to provide all these things, and still lose a child's heart?

2. How do you want it to be when that day comes for you?

Objective 2: *To see romance as the keystone to reaching the goal.*

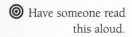 Have someone read this aloud.

Various approaches have been used for winning a child's heart, including training, discipling, and mentoring. More recently, the word *shepherding* has come into use through a book by Ted Tripp. These words actually describe different kinds of relationships common between parents and children. They seem to overlap in practice, but there are significant differences.

Resource: Tedd Tripp, Shepherding a Child's Heart.

Training is essentially the development of habits. The key concept is molding the will without breaking the spirit. This goal is especially important for young children, not only for their character development but also for their safety and well-being. Training also instills skills and behavior essential for living in society.

Discipling is teaching spiritual truths and/or academic knowledge. The goal is the personal mastery of spiritual disciplines and acquisition of knowledge through a course of study that lasts for a limited time. Discipling is driven by the discipler's agenda; respect for the discipler is required.

Mentoring is caring for, helping, and supporting a person toward maturity. It is practical exposure to all relevant areas of life and is more relationship focused than content focused. It is usually a long-term commitment and process that does not require a specific curriculum. Respect, and a natural compatibility or attraction, are necessary.

Shepherding is the blending of discipling and mentoring in the context of parenting. It balances behavior training with heart training, showing a child how to know God and the true nature of reality. It infects children with a worldview that is focused on glorifying God and enjoying Him forever. Shepherding leads a child on a path of discovery, discernment, and wisdom.

In summary, **training** deals with the development of proper behavior and good habits; **discipling** emphasizes knowledge and disciplines; **mentoring** emphasizes the application of these to life; and **shepherding** includes them all with a focus on changing the heart, not just the behavior.

These approaches are foundational to the winning of a child's heart, but they are of little value if the child does not develop a heart after God. This happens through romancing, which links the essential components so that, when the time comes, the child chooses God and His way of wisdom. How parents can partner with God in facilitating this choice is the subject of this manual (and the book).

The process involved can be compared to building an arch, an amazingly strong architectural structure. The foundation is faith in God through Christ (salvation). The blocks of the arch, which form the vertical pillars, include training, discipling, mentoring, and shepherding, plus other components such as the spiritual disciplines of confession, fellowship, prayer, study, worship, celebration, silence, solitude, sacrifice, and service. (See the illustration at the end of chapter 8, *Romancing Your Child's Heart.*)

Keystone of the Arch

The keystone of the arch is romance. Although each block is essential, the most important is the keystone because without it the arch will collapse. As with an arch made of stone, the wedge-shaped keystone redirects all the forces in the arch back to the foundation, connecting the components to each other through what engineers call "compressive force."

In the same way, a heart that has been romanced to God links all the components of the child's spiritual life to the foundation, faith in Jesus Christ.

Activity

Using the graphic and instructions at the end of this chapter, build an arch of wood, cardboard, or Styrofoam and bring it to the session. Ask several people to help you assemble this structure. Then, after you have discussed the structural integrity of this form and explained why it stands so strong, pull out the keystone.

Then try to replace the keystone without the other stones there to support it.

Reflection/Discussion

1. Is building the "arch of faith" the most important goal of Christian parenting?

2. What insights come to mind about the relative importance of the keystone—romance—in the building of strong faith?

CONCLUSION: End the session with prayer.

PREPARATION FOR SESSION 2:

1. Read chapter 1, "Once upon a Childhood" and chapter 2, "Finding the Silver Bullet" in *Romancing Your Child's Heart*.

2. Select one of the following:

   __ Look through your childhood photo albums, watch old family movies and videos, read old letters.
   __ Travel back to your childhood home(s).

3. Identify, and be prepared to share about, people/things that drew you to God.

Instructions for Building the Arch

You can make the keystone arch of wood, cardboard, or Styrofoam. Wood is probably the most practical and durable, but will require woodworking tools. If you do not have access to tools, any wood shop or cabinet shop will supply the wood and cut out and sand the arch. If you use cardboard or Styrofoam you will need to glue multiple sheets together to achieve the required thickness of 4 inches. If you choose to make the arch have the rough dimensions of 15 inches by 15 inches.

The drawing of the arch in the manual can be enlarged to 15 inches by 15 inches and then used to trace the pattern onto the material. It is possible to cut this pattern out of each sheet of cardboard or Styrofoam before they are glued but as with wood a band saw or jig saw will make a much better cut and the blocks will fit perfectly together. Label the arch using a Magic Marker, paint brush, or printed labels. Remember to bring the keystone arch to all sessions. It will provide visual continuity as each session builds on the one(s) before.

Group Leader: Be sure to acquire in advance the cap and cloak needed during session 2. Also be aware that, because not everyone was effectively romanced to God as a child, during the session 2 sharing times, some group members may share seemingly negative things about their upbringing, while others will experience strong emotions. Be sure to affirm that you are studying this subject together, trying to learn as much as possible, and that sometimes the best lessons come from mistakes.

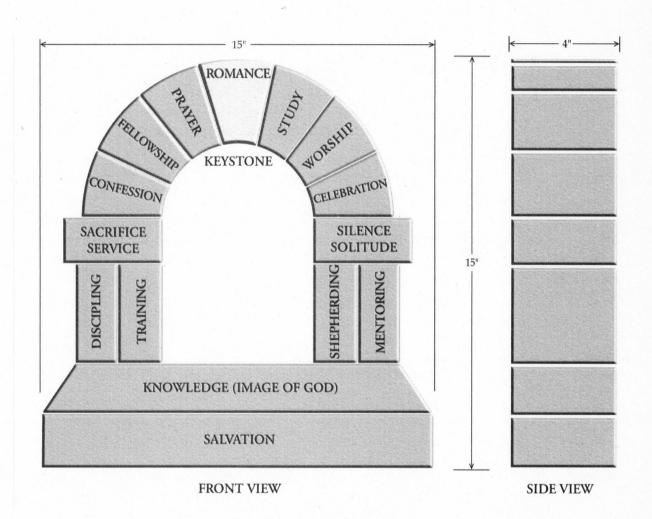

FRONT VIEW

SIDE VIEW

REMEMBERING HOW GOD WON YOUR HEART

Faded photos of our families, we read it in their eyes,
and hear a melody, that used to be, the music in our lives.

LYRICS FROM "OLD TRAILS," BY MONTE SWAN

In the summer of 2000, Karey and I spoke at Sandy Cove on Chesapeake Bay. The message of "Romancing Your Child's Heart" touched one of the fathers in a very special way. Toward the end of the week he shared his story with us.

 Have someone read this aloud.

"Until this week," Steve said, "I have misunderstood my father—never really appreciating him. He wasn't the kind of father who would play ball with me and do all those things the parenting books say a father should do. So I thought he had somehow failed me." As the tears began to flow, Steve continued, "But my father did pour his music into my life—it was all he knew. I never realized until now that when my father shared his first love—his passion—with me, he was romancing me to God the only way he knew how. He included me—trained me and taught me his music—and now he is so proud of my music. He was successful as a father because he won my heart for God by giving the finest part of himself to me."

Steve concluded, "I see it clearly now—the idea of the Larger Story—and I intend to do this for my children, to romance their hearts to God. I thought I was on track, focusing primarily on teaching them biblical truth and training them in proper behavior, but I was missing the true prize. I am going to enter the contest for their hearts."

Reflection/Discussion

1. **Reflect:** With which part of Steve's story can you most identify?

2. **Share:** How does this story broaden your perspective on the role your parents had in romancing you to God?

LEADER'S PRAYER: *Father, this session will no doubt be emotional. Help us see Your truth through our tears and laughter, and through the humor, drama, and tragedy of our stories. Thank You for this wonderful group of parents, intent on winning their children's hearts. We pray that all the words spoken and shared today will teach and encourage, ultimately leading our children to You. We ask now that You will guide us through Your Spirit.*
In Jesus' name, amen.

SESSION GOAL: **To help participants recall the way God romanced them to Himself.**

SESSION OBJECTIVES

The word remember occurs over three hundred times in the Bible.

1. To remember how God romanced you to Himself.

2. To share the story of how your heart was won.

Objective 1: To remember how God romanced you to Himself.

◎ Have someone read this aloud wearing a feathered cap or a green cloak.

My own heart turned toward God in my "Robin Hood" days. Later, when the world began to woo me away, my mother and father chose to fight for my heart, not by building a wall around me but by out-romancing the competition. They knew that the vast and lush beauty of nature had always mesmerized me, so they gave me freedom to explore it. A sense of wonder burned strong in my heart. I know now that it was God drawing me to Himself.

As a little boy, I spent countless hours in the creek or hiking through hardwood forests and boggy marshes near my childhood home. I scrambled on the rocks, chased the dragonflies, and climbed the hills. I became intimate with the work of God's hands, and this made me desire to know Him.

The Larger Story is described more fully in "Living the Larger Story," chapter 3 of Romancing Your Child's Heart.

My parents provided a safe place for me to grow—a home where fairy tales really did come true. Their relationship provided the solid bedrock upon which my security was built. Although their life together included its share of adversity and tragedy, they continued to trust God, and they never lost heart. They pressed on, protecting me with a hedge of hope and joy, and a genuine vision for God's Larger Story.

Unconditional love, grace, and my parents' faith in me quenched any rebellion before it arose in my heart. This was a crucial element—my parents' hearts were irresistibly beautiful. The image of God, projected through them, naturally drew me to my heavenly Father.

I also remember the family stories and the books they shared—so full of adventure, mystery, and happily-ever-afters—including Bible stories from the first book my mother ever read me cover to cover: *Marian's Big Book of Bible Stories.*

All these things inspired me, nourishing my dreams, aspirations, and visions by protecting and cultivating my creativity. When they encouraged me to design, to bring order from disorder and make things, I sensed a camaraderie with my Creator. I felt His image coming alive within me. I built tree houses, sculpted dinosaurs from creek clay, and whittled animals from black walnut. I played the trumpet, built my own basketball court, and fished with homemade tackle. My childhood was a whimsical romance in which my parents, through much sacrifice, won my heart for God.

Reflection/Discussion

1. What is your first reaction when you read/hear this story?

    __ This never happened.
    __ This must have happened, because nobody could make it up.
    __ I wish it had happened to me.
    __ I want to make something like this happen for my kids.

2. Identify strategic arenas that my parents used to win my heart:

    _____

    _____

    _____

    _____

Objective 2: To share the story of how your heart was won.

Now it's your turn. Everyone has (or is living) a story, and that story is part of the Larger Story that God has been telling forever. So nobody's story is more important than anyone else's. They're just all tied together—Steve's, yours, mine, and our children's.

The goal of this exercise is to enable you to recall how your heart turned toward God—when and how you felt that desire for Him, and what may have influenced its birth. As Christians we know that the Holy Spirit is the Source of this miracle in our hearts, but often He uses people in this process.

◎ Have someone read this aloud.

Note: Not all responses will describe fairy-tale childhoods. The bulleted list contains examples of what typically emerges from this exercise. Note that while each set of parents employed unique methods, usually focusing on one area of parenting to the exclusion of others, each child's heart was won even when there was no apparent strategy involved. Some will have been won by grandparents or outside mentors. With this in mind, imagine how much more effective parents can be when they have a strategy and use it properly!

Sharing/Discussion

Describe how your heart turned toward God—be specific about people, places, activities, etc.—but also be as brief as possible to give everyone who wishes to share a chance to do so. Have someone record the key points on a white board or chalkboard.

- Never talked about God but walked the walk.
- Never discussed the Larger Story—children left to figure it out on their own.
- Did not respect the child as a person.
- Pushed child to excel in many areas.
- Fulfilled only the spiritual duties—devotions and prayer.
- Was only winsome, fun, childlike.
- Had no personal relationship—relational vacuum.
- Focused on "no-this" or "no-that" criticisms.
- Strong sense of community at expense of everything else.

CONCLUSION

Conclude the session with sentence prayers thanking God for creating in you a desire for Him and asking Him to use you (not others by default) to win your child(ren) to Himself. The basic issue for Christian parents is whether or not they really want to become God's allies in a process that He will bring to pass, regardless. In other words, we can experience life's deepest joy by becoming co-romancers with God or we can miss the joy.

Going Deeper

1. Write a tribute to your parents and/or other adults, thanking them for their role in winning your heart for God. To find great ideas on how to do this, see: *Tribute and the Promise: How Honoring Your Parents Will Bring a Blessing to Your Life,* by Dennis Rainey with David Boehi; Thomas Nelson, 1997.

2. Journaling: Toward the back of this manual you will find blank pages, which you can use for recording your progress toward developing a vision and crafting a romance to win your child's heart. Most of these pages are blank, because each person's strategy will be unique. To reinforce what you've learned thus far, record your insights and the creative ideas you've gained from personal reflection and group discussion about yourself, God and faith, parenting in general, and creative ideas and strategies for romancing your child's heart.

PREPARATION FOR SESSION 3:

1. Read chapter 3, "Living the Larger Story," in *Romancing Your Child's Heart*.

2. If possible, read the book *Pollyanna* by Eleanor Hodgman Porter, published in 1913. This bestseller captures the truth of the Larger Story, especially through the "glad game."

Group Leader: In session 3, two activities need your attention:
1. A short clip will be shown (pulled out of the middle of a film that needs the whole story line in order to understand what is happening).
Suggestions: *Groundhog Day*—pickup truck crash; *Ever After*—bee scene; *Brigadoon*—ending; *Les Misérables*—river drowning scene.
2. The make-believe "campfire" situation at the end of the session will require some props, such as stones, sticks, lantern/flashlight.

LIVING IN THE LARGER STORY

There's a way of wisdom, and a way of fools.
And the way of wisdom is straight and true.
LYRICS FROM "STRAIGHT AND TRUE," BY MONTE SWAN

Once upon a morning, the prophet Elisha awoke to find that an army had surrounded the city with horses and chariots. Elisha's servant, Gehazi, trembled with fear at the sight of this enemy. In a state of panic he asked, "What shall be done?" Elisha said, "Those who are with us are more than those who are with them." You can imagine the look on Gehazi's face as he probably thought, *I don't see anyone with us.* Elisha asked God to let Gehazi see the spiritual reality—the Larger Story. Then Gehazi saw the hills around them full of heaven's horses and chariots of fire. I can just picture his eyes opening wide and his jaw dropping in amazement. Immediately his outlook changed. Joy and hope replaced the fear and despair in his heart, as the invisible became visible (see 2 Kings 6:15–17).

◎ Have someone read this aloud.

Reflection/Discussion

1. When you face a difficult situation, do you normally react like Gehazi or Elisha?

2. Describe how you feel when you are around believers who live, as Elisha did, in the Larger Story.

If you seek her [wisdom] as silver, and search for her as for hidden treasures; then you will understand the fear of the LORD, and find the knowledge of God.
(Proverbs 2:4–5)

LEADER'S PRAYER: *Father, we ask that Your truth will be spoken today and that we will gain more insight into this romance of Christ. Help us grasp the idea of the way of wisdom and walk it as You so passionately desire us to.*
In Jesus' name, amen.

SESSION GOAL: **To help participants recognize that the adventure of living in the Larger Story will irresistibly attract their children to its Author.**

SESSION OBJECTIVES

1. To understand the meaning of living in the Larger Story.

2. To understand that the way of wisdom is the ultimate hunting trip.

Objective 1: To understand the meaning of living in the Larger Story.

◎ Have someone read this aloud.

Some people see me as a hopeless optimist, out of touch with reality. They call me "Pollyanna," which is okay with me, because I've read the book *Pollyanna*, which was a national bestseller back in 1913. It's a marvelous tale of how a little orphan girl, with every right to be bitter, transforms an entire New England town by teaching the "glad game" she learned from her minister father before he died. Essentially, the glad game's goal is to find a way to be glad for whatever happens. Here's a segment from the book:

> "Why, it's a game. Father told it to me and it's lovely," rejoined Pollyanna. "Why, we began it on some crutches that came in a missionary barrel."
>
> "*Crutches!*" [replied Nancy, the maid].
>
> "Yes. You see I'd wanted a doll, and father had written them so; but when the barrel came the lady wrote that there hadn't any dolls come in, but the little crutches had. So she sent 'em along as they might come in handy for some child, sometime. And that's when we began it."
>
> "Well I must say I can't see any game about that," declared Nancy, almost irritably.
>
> "Oh yes; the game was to just find something about everything to be glad about—no matter what 'twas," rejoined Pollyanna, earnestly. "And we began right then—on the crutches."
>
> "Well, goodness me! I can't see anythin' ter be glad about—gettin' a pair of crutches when you wanted a doll!"
>
> Pollyanna clapped her hands. "There is—there is," she crowed. "But *I* couldn't see it either, Nancy, at first," she added, with quick honesty. "Father had to tell it to me."

"Well then, suppose *you* tell *me*," almost snapped Nancy.

"Goosey! Why, just be glad because you *don't—need—'em!*" exulted Pollyanna, triumphantly. "You see it's just as easy—when you know how!"

"Well, of all the queer doin's!" breathed Nancy, regarding Pollyanna with almost fearful eyes.

"Oh, but it isn't queer—it's lovely," maintained Pollyanna enthusiastically. "And we've played it ever since. And the harder 'tis, the more fun 'tis to get 'em out; only—only—sometimes it's almost too hard—like when your father goes to Heaven, and there isn't anyone but a Ladies' Aid left.

"You see, when you're hunting for the glad things, you sort of forget the other kind—like the doll you wanted, you know.

"Most generally it doesn't take so long," sighed Pollyanna, "and lots of times now I think of them *without* thinking, you know. I've got so used to playing it...."

Pollyanna's father had left her a rich legacy, a perspective that would carry her forward no matter what might happen. Together, they named it the glad game.[1]

Believe me, I know it's not always easy (Pollyanna even admits this from time to time in the book) to maintain an attitude of gratitude in the face of difficult circumstances. In fact, it's *impossible* to maintain this perspective unless you believe that the story of your own life is part of a Larger Story about a loving God and His people, who see with the eyes of faith.

My coauthor lost his first son—three years old at the time—in 1978. Right now he's working on a book entitled *Joy Again*. How could he use such a devastating loss to minister God's healing through the years? "I can be joyful or thankful only because I know there is a Larger Story," he says, "the one that ends happily ever after, in heaven, where we'll finally understand what may not make sense today."

I came close to this kind of loss when my three-year-old, Travis, had a bout with viral meningitis. I must admit that the approach my wife, Karey, took taught me a lot. While I worried and fretted, she calmly took care of Travis, hour after hour, day after day, because she was confident that God was in control, and that He would make it turn out for our best. She chose to view this crisis with the eyes of faith, which was hard for me until I also found peace by realizing that I could trust God with our son's life.

I share these examples to make it clear that a Pollyannaish perspective is not denial of reality, but a deliberate choice to take a God's-eye view. This choice allows us to see what my coauthor likes to call "reality with a big R," and which I like to call the "Larger Story." That is, God's work in and through the events of our lives. You can call it "playing

Rejoice always...in everything give thanks; for this is the will of God in Christ Jesus for you. (1 Thessalonians 5:16, 18)

Pause and read the next four paragraphs silently before discussing the questions.

Now faith is the substance of things hoped for, the evidence of things not seen. (Hebrews 11:1)

the glad game" or "walking the walk" or whatever you choose, but my conviction is that we all do choose, on a daily basis, how we will view life. Choosing God's viewpoint communicates faith—the "evidence of things not seen"—to everyone around us, especially our children.

Choose one of the following activities.

Activity

Role-play in a group setting: Four "players" from two families (two parents, two kids each).

Situation: As a result of a major storm in the middle of the winter, you lose power in your all-electric house for a full day. The storm occurs just before supper on Friday night. Role-play the situation twice, with two sets of players.

Family 1: This is an extreme inconvenience and a major catastrophe—they can't watch their rented video, the toilet's only going to flush once, etc.

Family 2: This is a great opportunity to camp out in their own living room—using their somewhat neglected camp stove, lantern, sleeping bags, and maybe even a tent.

Reflection/Discussion

1. As a group, discuss which of the two family interactions you would rather have in your own family's "album of memories" ten years from now.

2. Privately, recall a situation similar to the one just role-played. What would you change if you had it to live over again? (Be kind to yourself—wisdom is always easier in retrospect.)

3. Record in your journal any insights or goals arising from this reflection and/or discussion.

Film Clip

View a segment from the middle of a movie and try to guess what is going on *based only on what you have seen.* Discuss how difficult it is, without the context of the Larger Story, to understand the meaning of what you've seen.

Reflection/Discussion

1. How is the problem of discerning a movie's outcome from a short clip similar to the challenge of walking by faith, not by sight?

2. If you were observing your own family's story over the past few months, would you be satisfied with the plot?

3. What would you change in order to align the script more completely with your true view of reality? Record these things in your journal.

Objective 2: To understand that the way of wisdom is the ultimate hunting trip.

In the late 1970s I tried hunting elk with a bow and arrow in northern Arizona. For a week, two partners and I engaged in what turned out to be an exercise in futility—emphasis on exercise. Keep in mind that elk can smell, see, and hear much better than humans—plus they can walk faster than I can run. Each night the three of us would sit around the campfire, sharing stories about elk sign. Each would contribute whatever "valuable" observation he'd made during the day's hunt. Together, we assembled these pieces of data and plotted them on topographic maps, trying to reconstruct the larger story—the "Way of the Wapiti" (*wapiti* is Shawnee for *elk*) on that particular mountain. Before we hit the sack each night we had constructed our hunt strategy for the next day by factoring the direction of the wind, moisture, temperature, and phase of the moon.

We were participating in an activity central to what it means to be human—not so much hunting elk as sharing a quest, an adventure, a search. It was a treasure hunt, and the prize was not bagging an elk, for that would end the hunt. It was the process, together with the fellowship of comrades. By the way, we never harvested an elk but we had numerous close encounters and lost many arrows. I'm sure the elk still tell romantic tales about three crazy humans, dressed like bushes, showing up in the most unpredictable places for a week, one aspen-gold September many elk-generations ago.

In Proverbs, the search for wisdom is described as "the way of wisdom." The word *way* describes the "walk of faith." "The way" was the first name applied to the movement that eventually became known as Christianity. The way of wisdom is a quest analogous to my Arizona hunt, where the goal is actually the search itself…for clues and glimpses—"sign" and "tracks" of God, whom the poet Francis Bacon called "the hound of heaven." As Christian parents we fit these clues, like pieces of a puzzle, into the Larger Story and apply what we have learned to life, creating a strategy through our moral imagination.

True fellowship is doing this in community. In Arizona, my partners and I gathered around a campfire. In the same way, parents can gather their families around the dining room table. Children witnessing the passion of the drama, and our childlike hope during this process, will be drawn to it and to its Source.

"Wisdom," Proverbs asserts, "is pleasant to your soul." But wisdom is not static or an end in itself; it is described as a "good path," to be followed through resourcefulness: "Discretion will preserve you; understanding will keep you" (See Proverbs 3:15;

Read the next section silently.

My son, if you receive my words, and treasure my commands within you, so that you incline your ear to wisdom, and apply your heart to understanding; yes, if you cry out for discernment…then you will understand the fear of the LORD, and find the knowledge of God. (Proverbs 2:1–3, 5)

2:10–11). Biblical wisdom is a way of living. It is not something we finally achieve in our old age, nor is it the prize at the end of the race; it is living creatively and resourcefully in the Larger Story.

 Have someone read this aloud.

The way of wisdom (the Larger Story, the glad game) is not a stuffy, boring religious concept. It is the literal and spiritual path that almighty God has designed for each of us to walk through this life. As we walk, we should do so with bated breath and trembling excitement. We will look at the world with wide-eyed wonder and awe, and we will understand the implications of the central truth of the Larger Story—that "in Him we live and move and have our being" (Acts 17:28).

As our children see us bowing before God and serving others, tremors will pass down their spines, because they will begin to suspect that God is really real. The intimate presence of the Holy Spirit, unleashing the power of a personal God in our lives, will allow our children to witness awe-inspiring encounters. They will comprehend the passionate love God has for them, and will be irresistibly drawn to Him as they respond to the romance. They will greet each new day with wonder and joy as each new page of the romance is turned. They will see that relationship is central in all we do.[2]

Activity

Using stones for a circle and a teepee of sticks, build a make-believe campfire in the middle of your group. Turn down the lights and use a lantern or flashlight for the campfire.

A campfire almost demands narration and response from those sitting around it. Everyone has a story as the circle of light and warmth draws us in out of the darkness. We feel far from the distractions of our urgent world. We are also not on a stage, expected to perform. We are just here, now, together. Campfires magically create a sense of camaraderie and community in the people encircling the fire, providing a setting where the deepest communication can occur, not merely through words but intuitively, through feelings—the connector of human hearts.

Discussion/Sharing

You have just come in from hunting—you've been searching for truth and the wisdom to know how to apply it in leading your family.

1. Share any of the "sign" you've seen, or the "tracks" you've been following, and what these are telling you.

2. What is your strategy for continuing the hunt?

3. Record significant observations (from your own experience or your comrades') in your journal.

4. Compose a prayer for greater discernment, strength, and courage to carry out the plan. Share any components of this prayer with your group (or your spouse) and then close with group prayer, presenting these requests together to the Lord.

PREPARATION FOR SESSION 4:

1. Read chapter 4, "The Dynamics of Story," in *Romancing Your Child's Heart*.

2. Bring your family photo album to session 4.

Just do it. How "successful" you are at hunting (for truth or anything else) is not the point. What really matters is that you are hunting—hunting in hope, for the pure joy of it—and that you take your child along and include him or her with your comrades "around the campfire." Camaraderie, not competition, is the way to win a heart.

Group Leader: Select a segment from a Focus on the Family *Odyssey* story to play during session 4. Don't forget to bring the tape player!

WOOING YOUR CHILD WITH STORY

I read the Bible as a story, because that's the way the Bible presents itself.
God has spoken to us in story, and we will do well to listen the way God has spoken.
And, in my opinion, if we read the Bible as anything but story,
we are fundamentally unbiblical.

DON HUDSON, *MARS HILL REVIEW*

One of the Bible's best-known stories takes place after King David committed adultery with Bathsheba and then ordered her husband left alone in the thickest part of battle so he would be killed.

◎ Have someone read this aloud.

And when her mourning was over, David sent and brought her to his house, and she became his wife and bore him a son. But the thing that David had done displeased the LORD. Then the LORD sent [the prophet] Nathan to David. And he came to him, and said to him: "There were two men in one city, one rich and the other poor. The rich man had exceedingly many flocks and herds. But the poor man had nothing, except one little ewe lamb which he had bought and nourished; and it grew up together with him and with his children. It ate of his own food and drank from his own cup and lay in his bosom; and it was like a daughter to him. And a traveler came to the rich man, who refused to take from his own flock and from his own herd to prepare one for the wayfaring man who had come to him; but he took the poor man's lamb and prepared it for the man who had come to him." So David's anger was greatly aroused against the man, and he said to Nathan, "As the LORD lives, the man who has done this shall surely die! And he shall restore fourfold for the lamb, because he did this thing and because he had no pity." Then Nathan said to David, "You are the man!" (2 Samuel 11:27–12:7)

Reflection/Discussion

Imagine that you're the prophet Nathan walking up the steps to the throne room. The Lord has sent you to deliver a message to the king—a message you're quite confident he won't be happy to hear.

1. What are you thinking?

   __ Wish I didn't have to do this.
   __ He really deserves a lightning bolt.
   __ This is going to take a mighty good sermon.
   __ I have to reach his heart somehow.

2. Why was the use of story more effective in this situation than straightforward condemnation might have been?

3. When you want your child to internalize something very important, which of the following approaches have been most effective?

   __ yelling (raising the emotions)
   __ withdrawal (the cold shoulder)
   __ threatening (instilling fear)
   __ bribing (rewarding)
   __ reasoning (use of logic)
   __ repetition (rote training)
   __ whispering
   __ using stories or other creative methods
   __ other: _____

4. Being ruthlessly honest, prioritize the above list according to your normal parenting MO (mode of operation).

5. Reprioritize the list according to how you would really like to parent. Record your thoughts in your journal.

Have someone read the setting description, then discuss your answer(s) to the question.

Share your responses to the above, then reflect privately on the next two questions, recording your answers in your journal.

We can tell our children *what to do*, or *how to do* something. We can teach them morals and rules. But what we say is likely to go in one ear and out the other, unless we give them handles by which to grab the meanings we wish to communicate. Good stories carry the freight of truth without moralizing. The best stories show us God's reality, developing within us a thirst to experience it, not just know about it. Stories enable us both to feel and to understand, and this empowers us to live well. Stories do not storm our hearts, they sneak past the screens and filters of our rational minds. Instead of being stored like bare facts in the files of our intellect, stories infect our spirit. They touch, open, penetrate, and move our hearts, because they bring meaning to life, and meaning is essential to being truly human.

Read the following paragraph silently.

LEADER'S PRAYER: *Father, help us understand story, the subject of this session— and why You designed it in our minds, our thoughts, and our consciousness. Help us realize that story is the language of the divine—the language You use to reach beyond our minds to our hearts. Help us comprehend the power of story to win our child's heart for You.*
In Christ's name, amen.

SESSION GOAL: To help participants use story to help romance their child's hearts to God.

I will open my mouth in a parable. (Psalm 78:2)

All these things Jesus spoke to the multitude in parables. (Matthew 13:34)

SESSION OBJECTIVES

1. To understand the unique power of story in romancing a child's heart.

2. To embrace fairy tale as best representing the Larger Story.

Objective 1: To understand the unique power of story in romancing a child's heart.

Chuck Bolte, the executive producer of the popular *Odyssey* radio stories, told me that his mission was to produce good stories that, in themselves, carried God's truth to the listener via the "theater of the mind." He had faith in the power of story as a ministry tool, and he believed that stories built around sermonettes do not reach the heart. He operated on this premise: "Truth emanates out of story, and not the reverse." Children learn truth from the *Odyssey* stories not because someone says they *ought* to listen, but because they *want* to listen.

◎ Have someone read this aloud.

Dr. James Dobson—the originator of the *Odyssey* idea—had both a nostalgic desire for old-time radio and a belief that radio drama could compete with Saturday morning cartoons. Virtually no one agreed with him, believing that this generation of kids could only be reached by fast-paced visual stimulation. But a good story can reach the heart like nothing else can.

Play a segment from an *Odyssey* tape.

Activity

1. Why do children love these stories?

2. Why do adults love these stories?

◎ Have someone read this aloud.

Well-crafted stories capture our attention, ambush our hearts, and then dazzle us with beauty and resolution. They are more than just a series of logical ideas or a grammatically correct arrangement of words. In fact, sometimes stories don't involve words at all.

Reflection/Discussion

1. Check each of the arenas below where stories can be found:

   __books __films __paintings __theatre __sculpture __symphony
   __pop music __crafts __photo albums __nature __poetry __athletics

2. Which of these can be used to communicate truth to your child's heart?

Objective 2: To embrace fairy tale as best representing the Larger Story.

◎ Have someone read this aloud.

Once upon a time there was a great and powerful king who loved a humble maiden, one of his subjects. Although this great king commanded legions, and princes far and near trembled at the mere thought of his displeasure, his mighty heart languished in love for this common girl. The king knew he could summon his subject to the castle, adorn her with royal robes, and shower her with marvelous gifts—even against her will, for no one dared resist him. Surely she would be impressed, pleased, possibly even happy. But the only thing that mattered was beyond even the king's control and command: Would she love him? And how would he know for sure, for she might feign love even if she lived in fear, just as many of his subjects feigned fealty because they had no other choice.

No, he reasoned, *she must choose me freely, or her love may prove untrue. I could go to her cottage and make my love known. But even then she might feel constrained, compelled. May it never be! I will descend, disguised, and make myself nothing in order to win my lady's heart.*

So the great king humbled himself, laid aside his crown, his robes, and his rights, took on the appearance of a commoner, and headed for a certain forest cottage to romance a certain maiden on her own turf and terms.[3]

1. In a group setting, identify the story's message.

2. Why is this such an effective way to communicate it?

A traditional fairy tale involves clearly defined characters engaged in conflict between good and evil. The story has a beginning, follows a linear arrow of time, and has an end. Good ultimately triumphs, and the characters live happily ever after. This pattern is "Christian," in contrast with the modern story that often follows a circular, relativistic path leading to nonresolution.

Children need fairy tales as a part of their moral training, for this type of story mirrors the Larger Story, and impresses that pattern in their minds as they participate in the story in their imagination. This is important practical training for the challenges they will face as adults, because it gives them a template for discerning truth from lies, of which we all know they'll hear plenty.

We all want that kind of transfer from the imagination to actual life for our children. But to achieve the goal we must keep in mind that children learn almost nothing from abstractions and almost everything from stories, because they internalize them—they *become* the characters in the story. When a story's conflict is resolved, new insight is gained. When a character fails, lessons are learned that will provide guidance when the child faces adult ambiguities.

When good triumphs over evil, a seed is planted that will someday grow into faith that God is good and can be trusted. When the characters live happily ever after, the child is connected, if only for an instant, with the Larger Story of which fairy tales are but a mere reflection—the story that promises eternal happiness for those who come to God by faith.

For children raised this way, their whole childhood and adolescence has been a rehearsal for living as adults in our culture. They are practiced in the art of living in story— which we hope and pray will include the Larger Story that is scripted and choreographed by God. They do not need to search for meaning; they have found it already. They become preoccupied, enthralled, fascinated, captivated by the Larger Story, like deer panting after the water brooks—people after God's own heart.

Activity

Everyone has a story. We all live *in a story* in one way or another. And all our stories are part of the Larger Story. To illustrate this, open your family photo album and share with the group the part of His story that you see on one of its pages.

◎ Have someone read this aloud.

It is only the story...that saves our progeny from blundering like blind beggars into the spikes of the cactus fence. The story is our escort. Without it we are blind. (Chinua Achebe, Anthills of the Savannah)

A Word of Encouragement

You can learn to tell stories. We'll come back to this later in session 10, "Wielding the Tools of Romance." But here are some ideas for now:

◎ Invite interesting people for dinner and ask them questions (and let your children ask, too) about the story of their lives, especially how God has led them through it all.

◎ Listen to audio tapes with your children, like the *Odyssey* series from Focus on the Family. Talk about the characters and the plot, without moralizing.

◎ Read historical fiction, or biographies of great people, aloud.

◎ Watch and discuss quality videos and great films.

◎ Write and act out Scripture-based dramas or plays. For example, try modernizing the Parable of the Prodigal Son.

The only thing you can do wrong is not try. Your worst effort will still be better than none at all. Children are not as much concerned about perfection as authenticity. The fact that you are trying to connect shows your love and draws you into the Larger Story. In the end, this is what they will remember, when all the dust has settled and all the books are closed.

CONCLUSION: End the meeting with prayers of thanksgiving for God's grace in allowing your story to be a part of His Larger Story.

PREPARATION FOR SESSION 5:

1. Read chapter 5, "Out-Romancing the Competition," in *Romancing Your Child's Heart.*

2. Review your journal to see if it is up-to-date.

Group Leader: Bring to session 5 the largest and loudest Hawaiian shirt you can find.

COMPETITION FOR YOUR CHILD'S HEART

[Satan decided] to wound God as deeply as possible
by stealing the love of his beloved through seduction.

BRENT CURTIS

Many Christian parents would describe their efforts to win their child's heart as engagement in spiritual warfare. But the romance of a child's heart is more like a beauty contest than open warfare. My parents' strategy was to out-romance the competition.

◎ Have a woman read this aloud.

In my early teens, my artistic side was expressed in a passion for clothes. I loved to dress in a unique—some might even have said outrageous—way, including stunningly colorful Hawaiian shirts. Every time a girl passed by she would hum "Aloha" to me. I loved it.

◎ Have the man wearing THE SHIRT read this aloud.

Mom drew the line at black leather jackets, but she was still my kindred spirit. She took me to stores in downtown Milwaukee, far away from where we lived, where I could find my "cool threads." Instead of fighting me tooth and nail about every item of clothing—which most of my friends' mothers were doing—Mom fought for my heart and won, hands down. I think she viewed this part of the contest for my heart as a costume party. Come to think of it, I always did take first place at costume parties, whenever she handmade my costume.

Reflection/Discussion

1. What is your reaction to this radical strategy of my mother?

2. What are the "Hawaiian shirts" and "black leather jackets" of today?

LEADER'S PRAYER: *Father, we all love our children and try so hard to protect them from evil and the spiritual war raging all around us. Help us see that there is a ceaseless competition for their hearts, and realize that competition implies a competitor—a rival—another suitor for their souls. Please speak through our words.*
In Jesus' name, amen.

Put on the whole armor of God, that you may be able to stand against the wiles of the devil. (Ephesians 6:11)

SESSION GOAL: To help participants realize that Satan is a suitor competing with us in the romance for our child's heart.

SESSION OBJECTIVES

1. To realize that there is a "beauty" contest going on for your child's heart.

2. To know the geography of the three parenting realms in which this contest takes place.

3. To understand that only parents who are proactive in this contest stand any chance of winning.

Objective 1: To realize that there is a "beauty" contest going on for your child's heart.

◎ Have someone read this aloud.

A few months before I was born, my dad met a stranger who was new to our small midwestern town. From the beginning, Dad was fascinated and soon invited him to live with our family. The stranger was quickly accepted and was around to welcome me into the world a few months later.

As I grew up I never questioned his place in our family. Mom taught me to love the Word of God. Dad taught me to obey it. But the stranger was our storyteller. He would weave fascinating tales. Adventures, mysteries, and comedies were daily conversations. He could hold our whole family spellbound for hours each evening. Mom and Dad never needed to tell their stories or read to us because he was always there. He dazzled and romanced us. We gave him nearly all our free time.

He was like a friend to the whole family. He took Dad, Bill, and me to our first major league baseball game. He was always encouraging us to see the movies, and he even introduced us to several movie stars.

The stranger was an incessant talker. Dad didn't seem to mind, but sometimes Mom would quietly get up—while the rest of us were enthralled with one of his stories of faraway places—and go to her room, read her Bible, and pray. I wonder now if she ever prayed that the stranger would leave. My father ruled our household with certain moral convictions, but this stranger never felt an obligation to honor them. Profanity, for example, was not allowed in our house—not from us, our friends, or adults. Our longtime visitor, however, used occasional four-letter words that burned my ears and made Dad squirm. To my knowledge the stranger was never confronted.

My father was a teetotaler who didn't permit alcohol in his home—not even for cooking. But the stranger felt he needed exposure and enlightened us to other ways of life. He offered us beer and other alcoholic beverages often. He made cigarettes look tasty, cigars manly, and pipes distinguished. He talked freely (much too freely) about sex. His comments were sometimes blatant, sometimes suggestive, and generally embarrassing. I know now that my early concepts of the man/woman relationship were influenced by the stranger. As I look back, I believe it was only by the grace of God that the stranger did not influence us more. Time after time he opposed the values of my parents. Yet curiously, he was seldom rebuked and never asked to leave.

More than thirty years have passed since the stranger moved into our home. But if I were to walk into my parents' den today, you would still see him sitting over in the corner, waiting for someone to listen to him talk and watch him draw his pictures. His name? We always called him "TV."

Reflection/Discussion

1. What do you think is the point of this story?

    __ TV is the most evil invention ever.
    __ The "force" of TV is stronger than most people realize.
    __ Even fathers with good intentions and values can be mesmerized
       by the TV.
    __ The mother should have protested.
    __ The story isn't really about TV. It's about _____.

2. The other suitor can slip in and court a child's heart without parents knowing it. If the parents in this story had realized what was happening, what might they have done to out-romance the other suitor?

Through time and experience we discover that everywhere we go is "holy ground" and everything we do is "sanctified action." The jagged line dividing the sacred and the secular becomes very dim, indeed, for we know that nothing is outside the realm of God's purview and loving care.[4]

Objective 2: To know the geography of the three parenting realms in which this contest takes place.

 Have someone read this aloud.

There are three realms in which we must compete with the other suitor, Satan, in the contest for our children's hearts—the empirical, rational, and spiritual realms. As you hear the descriptions of the three realms, list in your journal specific examples of the competition as you are experiencing it (or expect that you may).

Empirical Realm

The empirical realm is the concrete world: time, space, and matter—things that can be observed, measured, and experienced. Satan's strategy is to saturate parents with these things so they seldom have the energy to compete with him. Even when they do compete, he claims this world as his own and is successful, not only in counterfeiting but also in monopolizing for his own evil purposes the beauty, wonder, and mystery of the things God has made.

Activity

Role-play: Have four volunteers role-play (two parents, two kids) the following situation: As a group, you are trying to find *one night each week* to spend at home together, just enjoying each other's company (however you define that). Johnny plays soccer, basketball, and baseball, and Jenny does drama and gymnastics. Both are members of the church youth group, part of the youth worship band, and members of the Bible quiz team. Dad is a deacon and the Sunday school superintendent, and he bowls in a church league during the winter. Mom teaches piano, is in the weaving guild, and plays organ for Sunday worship. They attend a weekly small group on *Romancing Your Child's Heart.*

1. What has to happen to accomplish the goal?

2. Is the "cost" too high?

Rational Realm

 Have someone read this aloud.

The rational realm is the immaterial world—its structure, form, and pattern as understood by our minds—including categories, ideas, logic, and our perception of knowledge, truth, and reality. Satan loves to entertain and amuse. (The word *amuse* means "not to think.") In other words, Satan uses a child's myriad amusements to produce a person content not to think. Alternatively, if they can think, he will try to convince them to be philosophical skeptics—cynical rationalists—by overwhelming them with secular ideas and deceptive logic, using the youth subculture to pressure them to conform. He also applies pressure from the adult world by exposing them, as early as possible, to a variety of moral dilemmas beyond their capacity to understand.

Activity

Role-play this situation between parent and teen: The date is September 18, 2001. The teen has come home from social studies class, promoting his/her teacher's suggestion that perhaps the terrorists had good reason for their actions.

After the role-play, discuss:

1. How can you better prepare to engage your child in meaningful dialogue about issues like this?

2. What would you want to accomplish? Check all that apply:

    __ Win the argument.
    __ Connect what's happening to the Larger Story (like a piece in the puzzle).
    __ Demonstrate the beauty of truly rational logic.
    __ Show respect for the child's reasoning process.
    __ Find out what that teacher said so you can discuss it with him or her.
    __ All of the above.
    __ Other: _____

Spiritual Realm

The spiritual realm includes our personality, which is our spiritual fingerprint, the essence of our being. Humans express who they are through communication, relationship, and fellowship...and building healthy relationships takes time. But even when we set aside time for nurturing our relationship with our children, Satan can sneak in and distract us. He contaminates the fellowship, sometimes by manipulating our agenda until it is at odds with our child's.

◎ Have someone read this aloud.

Reflection/Discussion

1. On a scale of 1 to 100, rate your spiritual relationship with your child, 1 being "almost nonexistent" and 100 being "soul mates."

0   10   20   30   40   50   60   70   80   90   100

2. What one thing could you do this coming week to improve this "score"?

3. Do only proactive parents stand any chance of winning this contest?

Objective 3: To understand that only parents who are proactive in this contest stand any chance of winning.

 Have someone read this aloud.

One of my friends told me how, looking back, he could see that his basic focus as a father was to provide for his family—a healthy environment, nice home, good education, clothes, food, etc. His basic assumption was that within the context of these things, plus exposure to the church, his children would, in effect, *raise themselves* to be good Christian adults. Instead, while he worked three jobs and his wife worked one, their kids each went his or her own way. Now, estranged from two of the three, he wishes he had it all to do over again. If so, he would approach parenting with a very different assumption.

Reflection/Discussion

Those who wish to do so may share a correction they intend to make in their assumptions. Close with prayer for each other.

1. What do you think my friend's assumption should have been?

2. How do you think this different assumption might have affected his choices?

3. To the degree that you have made similar assumptions, what might you do to correct your own path?

PREPARATION FOR SESSION 6:

Group Leader: Arrange for all the materials needed for activities in the next session (marbles, rope, and a blanket). Note the use of recorded music in one part of the session that depicts the love of God for us.

1. Read chapter 6, "The Watershed," in *Romancing Your Child's Heart*.

2. Record in your journal your own experience with "the watershed."

WATERSHED CHOICES

*What is often forgotten is that where there is
a watershed there is a line, which can be observed and marked.*

FRANCIS SCHAEFFER, *THE GREAT EVANGELICAL DISASTER*

I live near the Continental Divide—the Rocky Mountain backbone of North America. When you stand on the Divide above the timberline at Colorado's Loveland Pass (11,992 feet above sea level) and look east or west, peak after peak stretches out before you in a complex pattern of deeply carved glacial canyons.

In the late spring I've stood on a snowfield at the divide watching one rivulet of water flow east and another from the same snowfield flow west. This is how two droplets of water, once part of the same snowpack, can end up thousands of miles apart, in different worlds. The dividing line, in this case the Continental Divide, is called a watershed.

◎ Have someone read this aloud.

Activity

Construct a model of a mountain range by stringing a rope between two chairs and hanging some fabric, such as a blanket, over the rope. Then drop several marbles, one by one, on the ridgeline and observe what happens.

Reflection/Discussion

1. Imagine that these marbles are your children, and the ridgeline (watershed) is a decisive moment when each decides which way he/she will go in terms of faith.

2. Record in your journal any insights you gain from this exercise.

3. Share whatever you wish with the group.

LEADER'S PRAYER: *Father, during this session help us gain perspective on the romance of our children's hearts so we will see the lay of the land ahead—specifically, those watershed choices our children will make. We pray that this knowledge...this understanding...this view of the future will inspire us to do everything we can do to win our children's hearts—to enter the romance with resolve, determination, and passion. Help us now to learn from Your Spirit. In Jesus' name, amen.*

SESSION GOAL: **To help participants understand that effective romancing of a child's heart is crucial to the child's decision to follow Christ.**

SESSION OBJECTIVES

We love Him because He first loved us. (1 John 4:19)

1. To show that the child's decision is a watershed event of their life.

2. To show that God's romance of us is the original parenting model.

Objective 1: To show that the child's decision is a watershed event of their life.

Read the following silently, then discuss the questions.

Until a certain point in life, a child's thoughts and actions more or less depend on parental values and control. Parents stand like buffers, protecting their children from life-impacting choices, offering guidance and correction when necessary. As children near adulthood they begin to think more independently, choosing the way of wisdom or the way of folly. This watershed choice will have dramatic consequences, with the potential for life destinations that are worlds apart.

Proverbs 22:6 says: "Train up a child in the way he should go, and when he is old he will not depart from it." This verse is not only the key to this watershed event—its meaning is central to understanding the idea of the romance (see the book for an extended discussion of this). Our first desire as parents is that our children will receive Jesus Christ as their personal Savior. To me, the phrase "when he is old he will not depart from it [the way of wisdom]" implies that when a child has been started along the way, on reaching adulthood he or she will climb down from his or her parents' shoulders of faith and most likely choose to continue walking in the same direction.

But it is important to remember that this thought is expressed in a proverb. It therefore represents a general principle or axiom—not an absolute guarantee from God that every child raised in a "Christian" home will choose Christ when the time comes. Nor does it imply the parents' failure should their adult child choose to walk in what Jesus called the broad way that leads away from God. When this happens, as it sometimes does even in families where parents have done the best they could to instill a love for God in their children's hearts, it is a watershed event, revealing the heartset of the person and thus the probable trajectory of their whole life. If this situation is your own, it is good to remember that, while very few come to Christ after adolescence, 85 percent of "prodigals" will eventually realize that there really is a "Larger Story" and it is time to return to its Author, who patiently waits to welcome the prodigal home.

Until I was seven, I thought that my father was God. Once I discovered that this wasn't true, I began to look for the real God. A year later I asked the Lord into my life during an Awana meeting. As far as I was concerned, this decision was only natural, because my father had projected the image of God so accurately, genuinely, and positively that I wanted to know the Source of such love, personally. When I was a freshman in college, I reaffirmed this direction—that as an independent adult I would continue walking in the way of wisdom.

Reflection/Discussion

1. Describe to the group your own "watershed" experience, focusing specifically on the elements that most affected your decision.

2. Based on what you just heard (or shared), what insight have you gained into the process ordinarily used by God to win hearts to Himself?

Objective 2: To show that God's romance of us is the original parenting model.

Reflection/Discussion

While the group considers the following questions, play music that effectively depicts the love of God for us.

1. What is your reaction to the concept of God as the original romancer? Record your answer in your journal.

2. What words come to mind when you think of the most romantic person you know?

3. After taking 5–8 minutes to ponder these questions, share your answers.

◎ Have someone read
this aloud.

Resources:
Our Mutual Friend, a movie
based on a book of the same
name by Charles Dickens;
Reaching for the Invisible
God and The Bible Jesus
Read by Philip Yancey.

The relationship God desires with you and me is an affair of the heart—an eternally passionate romance written before time began. God's intense emotional love pulsates through the pages of Scripture. From the Psalms to the Prophets to the words and works of Jesus Himself, God's Word to His people says, "I love you."

In the Old Testament, God's approach to our hearts seems subtle, almost shy, even when He demonstrates His almighty power. God's people knew that He loved them, but for years they didn't even know His name. Then in the Person of Jesus, He shows up as the Hero of the story, having set aside His glory and power and come to rescue His bride...even at the expense of His own life. That, in my opinion, is the original romantic plot, which the greatest novels and films try to emulate.

Why does almighty God approach us so gently, but so sumptuously? Could even time have been created in order to show us the heart of a long-suffering, patient Lover—who gives us chance after chance after chance as He longs for us to come home?

When this divine romance of our hearts becomes real for us, when its passion penetrates past our minds to our souls and we allow it to move us, emotionally, then we are ready to romance our children's hearts to this same loving God. This process will not be difficult, for it will flow from your inner self, like a stream of refreshing, life-changing water, to everyone with whom you have a relationship—including your children.

Reflection/Discussion

1. Allow these thoughts of God to connect you with Him in a new way, then record your response in your journal.

2. Share whatever you wish with the group.

3. If He designed His story to draw us to Himself, what can we emulate as we seek to romance our children to Him?

◎ Group Leader:
Read the following text,
through the end of
the prayer.

A romancer is genuine and true, demonstrating such qualities as beauty, order, humor, peace, unconditional love, compassion, hope, enthusiasm, happiness, enchantment, and respect. A romantic person is a kindred spirit. "Big Story" romantics know that heaven is their destination, and so they cannot help but be full of smiles and joy. Such characteristics cannot be put on like a garment—they must come from the inside. If we want to romance our children's hearts, the truly pivotal watershed decision is our own. Do we yearn for a relationship with God that is characterized by firsthand knowledge and passionate love?

A mother once told me that she could not seem to "fill the gaps" in her parenting, but she had realized that they provide the opportunity for Christ to shine through so the child sees Christ, not the mother's failure. In truth, the "perfect" parent with no "gaps" is in a sense a Pharisee who will not allow Christ an opportunity to shine.

So, it's not a matter of where you worship, how long your prayer times are, or whether you have regular personal or family devotions. It's a matter of the heart. And it's a matter of what you want. Revelation 3:20 depicts Jesus as waiting outside a heart's door to come in and have fellowship with whomever will open that door to Him: "Behold, I stand at the door and knock. If anyone hears My voice and opens the door, I will come in to him and dine with him, and he with Me."

Will you open that door to Him? This is not so much a passage about how to be saved as how to have true fellowship with Him. I love the context—sitting around a table sharing a meal and sharing life. I trust this is what we all want for ourselves, and our children.

> **LEADER'S PRAYER:** *Lord, You know our hearts, so You know that we long to know You and Your love more personally and passionately—a love that heals all wounds, forgives all failures, and lifts every burden, filling each heart with joy and a peace that passes all understanding. May this day-to-day experience of Your love become a continual wellspring of love for others, especially the children You have placed within our care. Draw them to Yourself, through us, and may we always help and never hinder this result.*
>
> *In Jesus' name, amen.*

PREPARATION FOR SESSION 7:

Read chapter 7, "Requirements for Romance," in *Romancing Your Child's Heart.*

Group Leader: Be prepared to show the archery contest segment from a Robin Hood film. Also have paper on hand for the final activity.

Part Two

THE STRATEGY

INTRODUCTION
TO PART TWO

Sessions 7–12 focus on practical applications. Clarifying your vision and writing a romance strategy is the goal. The advantage of doing these sessions as a group is that you will generate a pool of creative ideas, valuable wisdom, and tactical experience to draw from as you compile, collaborate, and brainstorm together. This is a rich treasure to be mined and will also help prevent you from being blindsided by the competition. You will receive the bonus of encouragement and deepening friendships with the other parents in your group through the sharing, storytelling, and fellowship. So work together and gather material for your own strategy. It is also important to begin using a calendar to block out dates as you schedule special romance activities.

As mentioned earlier, the manual does not contain a simple parenting formula or checklist. It is designed to coach parents toward creation of their own romance vision and strategy. But a word of caution is required. Please do not let the process of writing your strategy become too consuming, lest you forget that God is your vision and your child's heart is the goal.

The three arenas of romance in which competition normally occurs are:

1. Parent's life—sessions 7–10.

2. Creation (nature)—session 11.

3. Creative image of God—session 12.

Each of these requires its own vision and strategy. Most likely there will not be enough time during the sessions for this task. You may not even be able to complete the discussion of each session's objectives in the allotted class or meeting time, and you will probably come up with additional objectives. Keep in mind that the list in the manual is not meant to be exhaustive; every family and every child is unique. One approach is to do a quick "brainstorm" on each objective, recording the material generated, for each family's use as they create their own vision and strategy. Another approach is to choose several objectives and concentrate on them during the session, leaving the rest of the objectives as homework. In other words, don't worry. Start when you can; end when you must. These sessions are just a part of a process that takes a parenting lifetime.

Group Leader: For each point of application we have included explanatory text and, in some cases, suggestions for specific activities, film clips, object lessons, and music to help stimulate sharing and brainstorming conversation. These are merely examples. It is strongly recommended that you personalize each point of application by finding your own props and personal stories to introduce and illustrate the points. This will help the participants to "own" the sessions, to be pulled into the process. To compete alone is difficult. To compete together is to incarnate the meaning of the biblical word *koinonia*, which means fellowship, sharing, or communion, obviously the best foundation for "community."

Session 7, "Preparing to Compete for Your Child's Heart," explains that you must prepare the soil of the heart for the seed of romance. Session 8, "The Challenge of Parental Incarnation," describes the central truth of the biblical model for winning a child's heart. Session 9, "The Profile of a Romancer," is about who we are, while session 10, "Wielding the Tools of Romance," focuses on what we do. Session 11, "Protecting the Sense of Wonder," encourages parents to protect and cultivate their child's sense of wonder through a challenging and exciting earth science "curriculum." Session 12, "Discovering the Creative Image," shows parents how to protect and cultivate the creative image of God, as expressed in their child, by helping their child discover and develop the creative domain(s) God has designed for them.

The commencement session, entitled "Following Through as Your Arrow Is Released," should be experienced in a retreat setting. It is focused on the follow-through process of releasing your child into the world. At its conclusion, participants will share their strategies and covenant together to support each other in this competition.

PREPARING TO COMPETE FOR YOUR CHILD'S HEART

I want to be your friend, not just your project.

Sheila Walsh

I competed in my first archery contest one beautiful sunny day in 1977. The setting was the White Mountains of Arizona. The result was embarrassment.

Several months before the shoot I had bought my first compound bow. After a few lessons and a little practice shooting at three hay bales stacked in my yard, I thought I was ready. I ended up shooting my first round with some of the best shooters in the state. By the end of that round I had lost or broken nine out of twelve of my brand-new XX75 anodized aluminum arrows. My arrows had stuck in trees, been shattered and bent as they slammed into rocks, and had flown off into the wild blue yonder, never to be seen again. The only thing I couldn't hit was the target.

I had no business entering that competition because I had not fulfilled the prerequisites. I hadn't read the directions or studied the mechanics of how a compound bow worked. I was not familiar enough with my bow to feel its rhythm. I was severely distracted by the famous archers who were watching me. I had never shot as many arrows in one day, so I was tired. My sights were off because I had dropped my bow. My shooting form was inconsistent. And because I had not waxed my string, it was fraying. All things considered, though I had the best equipment I could afford, the bow seemed to be working against me instead of "us" working as a team.

To truly compete requires not just excellent equipment but a well-thought-out strategy, including knowledge, training, discipline, conditioning, practice, and continuing refinement based on experience. These same prerequisites apply to any competition in which you want to contend for the prize.

Show a segment from the archery contest in a Robin Hood movie.

◎ Have the man wearing the Robin Hood cap or cloak from session 2 read this aloud, then discuss the questions.

Reflection/Discussion

1. Recall how you have prepared to compete for the "prize" of your child's heart.

2. How do you plan to proceed differently from this point on?

___ I will have a plan.
___ I will make it a priority.
___ I will learn as much as I can.
___ I will try, and if I fail, I will try again.
___ I will love my child(ren) by loving my spouse.
___ I will pray for myself and others with similar goals.
___ I will support and encourage others with similar goals.
___ Other: _____.

LEADER'S PRAYER: *Father, we have much to cover today. We ask that You will help us gather, from the wealth of experience in this room, practical ideas that we can use to develop our own strategies to win our child's heart for You. Help us prepare the soil of our child's heart so it will be receptive to the romance.*
In Jesus name, amen.

SESSION GOAL: **To help participants develop a written strategy for romancing their child's heart by examining the following prerequisites to romance:**

1. Become a student of your child.

2. Be sensitive to your child.

3. Show up for the romance.

4. Create margin for relationship.

5. Communicate heart-to-heart.

6. Shelter and protect your child's heart.

7. Demonstrate oneness with your spouse.

Do you not know that those who run in a race all run, but one receives the prize? Run in such a way that you may obtain it. And everyone who competes for the prize is temperate in all things.... Therefore, I run thus: not with uncertainty. Thus I fight: not as one who beats the air. But I discipline my body and bring it into submission, lest, when I have preached to others, I myself should become disqualified.
(1 Corinthians 9:24–27)

Activity

Except where otherwise noted, brainstorm responses to the question(s) following each prerequisite, with one group member recording (on a white board or something similar) insights as a list for each, without much discussion. After the session, participants will pick and choose, from this larger list, elements useful in the development of their personalized strategy.

Keep in mind that, while it will be great if you can get through all the prerequisites in one session, you can finish up on your own, if necessary.

The word brainstorming, *according to Webster's, is "a group problem-solving technique that involves the spontaneous contribution of ideas from all members of the group." The result should not be analysis but a rich reservoir of useful concepts from which to draw as you develop your strategy. Therefore, a few minutes on each question should suffice.*

Prerequisite 1: *Become a student of your child.*

It is virtually impossible to romance the heart of a person we do not know. We need to begin preparing for the romance by becoming students of our children. We must really come to know them. This kind of knowing requires ongoing research, observation, and data gathering, since children are continually growing and changing, developing and maturing. Whether our children are early or late bloomers, our task remains the same.

◎ Have someone read this aloud.

Brainstorm

What words or phrases come to mind when you think of being a student of your child?

Prerequisite 2: *Be sensitive to your child.*

Genuinely sensitive parents will listen, watch, and touch. They are capable of sensing minute changes because all their senses are tuned in to their child's physical, emotional, sociological, and spiritual status. They are aware of the child's needs and interests, joy or pain.

To become more sensitive, parents must pay attention. Make it a daily priority to concentrate consciously on each child. The other component is time—both quality time and quantity time. Quantity time is probably the most difficult for parents to spend in today's fast-paced world. But sometimes a child may need an entire day before they will share what is really on their heart. This is the rhythm of relationship.

◎ Have someone read this aloud.

Resources: The Way They Learn: How to Discover and Teach to Your Child's Strengths *by Cynthia Tobias.*

Brainstorm

What do you have to do to become more sensitive to your child?

> *Starter ideas:* Be aware of their interests, respect them as persons, embrace spontaneity, put aside assumptions, play "kid," plan activities so the child wonders, *What are my parents up to now?*

Prerequisite 3: Show up for the romance.

To achieve intimacy with a child, we must be there with our whole being, not just physically while our mind is distracted by concerns of yesterday or tomorrow. The greatest challenge for some parents in the romance of their child's heart is simply to show up for the romance. Fathers in particular can be overly focused and miss important moments and opportunities to be with their child.

◎ Have someone read this aloud.

Brainstorm

How do you remove the hindrances?

> *Starter Ideas:* Schedule fun time together, such as a talent night, game night, music night; seize God-given opportunities; be spontaneous; cook together; snowboard together; live in the present; and release irrelevant inhibitions by adopting the child's agenda rather than your own.

Prerequisite 4: Create margin for relationship.

Dr. Richard Swenson has diagnosed a virulent new disease that affects millions of people, called *The Overload Syndrome.* His prescription to counteract its effects and restore its victims is called *Margin.* He has written books with the above two titles, which bring hope and help to overloaded, overstressed, overextended, overburdened, overwhelmed parents.

He describes *margin* as the space between *load* and *limit.* It is where relationships happen—the relationships orchestrated by God. The modern world is characterized by progress that has brought pain. This is because human beings are finite, while progress continues to exponentially increase, trapping us in a vortex of insufficient time, money, and energy to accomplish our tasks. Our fatigue becomes exhaustion and we burn out.

◎ Have someone read this aloud.

Most relationships subsist on a chronic diet of leftovers. Instead, adopt a pro-relational philosophy of life, making sure that the integrity of relationships is protected. Create space in your calendar, your schedule, and your heart for the people [children] God has given you. (Taken from a conversation with Dr. Swenson)

Brainstorm

1. List the things in life that cause us to live without margin.

2. Think of ways to bring margin back into our lives.

Prerequisite 5: Communicate heart-to-heart.

Children need more than to *know* they are loved. They need to *feel* it. They need to touch our love, hold it in their hands, and feel that it is theirs. This gives them emotional wholeness. Children are sensitive and emotional beings—not cognitive adults. Their fund of knowledge is small and they communicate primarily through their feelings. The eyes of the heart determine how they perceive family members, their home, their friends, and the world.

◎ Have someone read this aloud.

Gary Chapman, Five Love Languages; *Ross Campbell*, How to Really Love Your Child.

Brainstorm

What do you want your children to "see" with the "eyes of their hearts"?

Prerequisite 6: Shelter and protect your child's heart.

Sometimes people have asked me: "Aren't you overprotecting your children?" To me, this question is illogical and fundamentally flawed. Of course I am overprotecting my children! I would never think of underprotecting them. I'd far rather be an "OPP" than a "UPP."

Our culture underprotects our children in the name of "preparation." This idea, too, is fundamentally flawed. Children are exposed to these things at younger and younger ages so that they may become "moral-dilemma literate." The world may believe that this is necessary preparation for adulthood, but in reality all it is doing is shredding their innocence. Protection should decrease, and preparation should increase, at appropriate age and developmental levels.

◎ Have someone read this aloud.

Discuss

Listed below are thirteen options for sheltering and protecting your child's heart. Try to prioritize the entire list, with number one being the hardest thing to implement.

__ Monitor friendships.

__ Supervise extracurricular activities.

__ Examine vacation plans.

Note:
If the group gets stuck, go on to prerequisite 7 and prioritize the list on your own, outside of group time.

__ Limit Internet access.

__ Eliminate unwholesome video games.

__ Move to a new community.

__ Simplify lifestyle.

__ Consider educational alternatives.

__ Eliminate TV.

__ Screen and limit home videos.

__ Keep communication open.

__ Recruit family and friends.

__ Make your home the gathering place.

Michael Medved and Diane Medved, Ph.D., Saving Childhood: Protecting Our Children from the National Assault on Innocence.

Prerequisite 7: Demonstrate oneness with your spouse.

Jay Kesler, former president of Youth for Christ, after many years of counseling young people, observed that the only common thread he found among successfully raised children was that their parents hugged each other. Parents who are not intimate friends, sharing the same goals for their family, do not ordinarily hug very much. Acting in a way that shows that your spouse is important creates security for your child. Positive rituals and habits such as "Love you, bye" or a kiss on the cheek before leaving for work are important to children.

Praying together with your spouse is one of the keys to developing and maintaining the intimacy in marriage that will draw children to Christ. Prayer isn't something we do as a means to an end. It is an attitude, part of who we are, a practical way to know God and be known by Him—in the present, where He constantly dwells.

As we parents walk the way of wisdom, inviting our children to walk with us, the most important thing is that we walk together, always aware that we have a divine companion walking with us and living in us. This is why prayer infuses the power of God into any relationship, especially marriage.

Brainstorm

How can you demonstrate oneness with your spouse?

Activity

During this session you have most likely amassed a rich treasure of creative ideas related to prerequisites to romancing your child's heart. These ideas can serve as a starting point for your personalized strategy, which will clarify over the next few weeks. Perhaps you've noticed that most of the ideas are made up of action verbs such as *plan, create, live, test, make, focus, look, talk, listen, watch, learn, touch, embrace,* and *show.* Fulfilling these requires living very intently even before you begin the romance.

For now, choose the prerequisite that needs your most urgent attention, and write that, anonymously, on a piece of paper. Have someone collect and then redistribute these papers, and close with prayer for one another, based on the piece you receive. Keep this "prayer request" throughout the week, praying for this person as the Lord brings him or her to your mind.

PREPARATION FOR SESSION 8:

1. In the journaling section at the back of this manual, develop your strategy for meeting the prerequisites to the romance of your child's heart. This may require difficult choices and changes. But "the prize" for which you strive is worth whatever it may cost. A personal strategy worksheet/outline is provided just before the journaling section to help you organize your thoughts.

2. Read chapter 8, "The Challenge of Parental Incarnation," in *Romancing Your Child's Heart.*

Group Leader: Be sure to bring to the next session all the props and supplies you'll need, such as a bag of cookies, gallon jug of rice or beans, plate, plastic glasses, and milk for the little party at the end.

THE CHALLENGE OF PARENTAL INCARNATION

*I must unlearn...the adult structure and the cumbered years
and you must teach me to look at the earth and
the heaven with your fresh wonder.*

JANE CLEMENT

When our friend Ray comes home from work, he enters the small world of each of his children. The second he walks in the door he lays aside his adult power and positions himself on their level—first on his knees, then eventually lying on the floor with his kids climbing all over him. Then, even if only five minutes of daylight remain, he will often grab a ball and take his kids outside to play. Because he knows that *right now* is really the only time he has available for his children.

Now...to envision this properly, you need to know that Ray holds the record for tackles as a linebacker for the former national champion Colorado Buffaloes. Yet this big man has a passion for small things, from miniature cars to shadow boxes. His fingers are the biggest in the house, but he can untie the tiniest knot on his kids' sneakers.

◎ Have someone read this aloud.

Reflection/Discussion

1. If it is difficult for you to enter your child's world, identify the reasons:

   __ It's scary to become vulnerable.
   __ It's hard to get my big body on the floor.
   __ It's risky to lay aside my power to control our agenda.

___ I've forgotten how.

___ It's out of character.

___ It's not dignified.

___ It's too open-ended.

___ Other: _____.

2. Identify potential benefits to both yourself and your child.

LEADER'S PRAYER: *Father, help us understand that "parental incarnation" is the keystone of the romance, central to the biblical model of parenting. Teach us this truth from Your Word and help us apply it with the passion You demonstrated with Your own Incarnation—as a baby, Your Son came to us, lived among us, died to save us. May we emulate His example as we love our children.*
In Jesus' name, amen.

Let this mind be in you which was also in Christ Jesus, who...made Himself of no reputation, taking the form of a bondservant, and coming in the likeness of men.... He humbled Himself and became obedient to the point of death, even the death of the cross.
(Philippians 2:5–8)

SESSION GOAL: **To help participants understand that parental incarnation is essential to winning their child's heart.**

SESSION OBJECTIVES

1. To understand what "be imitators of God" means in the context of parenting.

2. To understand that differences in romancing by mothers and fathers can help their child "see God" in stereo.

Objective 1: To understand what "be imitators of God" means in the context of parenting.

Ephesians 5:1–2

The apostle Paul exhorts believers to "be imitators of God, as beloved children, and [to] walk in love, as Christ also loved you" (literal translation). In a similar passage (see the verses in the margin) the apostle expounds poetically on the cost of Christ's love, preceding this description with an exhortation to all believers to adopt the attitude of Christ Jesus, who laid aside His divine power to become one of us, and who laid down His life so we might be redeemed.

When parents lay aside their adult status and power to enter their child's world, they *incarnate* the mind of our Servant-Savior, who romanced us to Himself by demonstrating God's character. He said, "He who has seen Me has seen the Father." A primary purpose of Jesus' life was to show us what God is like.

John 14:9

Our task as parents is similar—to so fully incarnate the character of God that our children will desire to follow Him and His way of wisdom. And His character is expressed in us through the fruit of His Spirit. We cannot produce this spiritual fruit by trying harder. It comes only by allowing the Spirit of God to live in and through us.

Just as Jesus deliberately chose to lay aside His power and enter our world, we must "step down" from the self-importance of our adult world to communicate and connect with our children. We must view their decisions and behavior in the context of their lives, not ours. Jesus was still God when He walked among us, and we will still be adults when we enter our children's world. But both incarnations have the same goal—connecting on the level of the heart for the purpose of redemption.

But the fruit of the Spirit is love, joy, peace, long-suffering, kindness, goodness, faithfulness, gentleness and self-control. (Galatians 5:22–23)

Reflection/Discussion

1. Jesus laid aside His power as God in order to win our hearts. What are some implications of this apparent paradox for Christian parenting in light of Paul's exhortation to be imitators of God?

   __ A child's heart cannot be taken by force.
   __ I can respect my child enough to risk rejection and trust God for the outcome.
   __ Love strong enough to win a heart is costly.
   __ The authority I seek can only be granted, not compelled.
   __ Humility is crucial in heart-winning.
   __ Incarnation results in maximum engagement.

2. Using a white board, create a list of attitudes involved in Christ's showing us what God is like.

   See John 3:16 and 15:13; 1 John 4:9–10.

3. Review this list and identify the costs involved in "incarnating" each attitude in your parenting.

Objective 2: To understand that differences in romancing by mothers and fathers can help their child "see God" in stereo.

One summer I mentored an eighteen-year-old boy. It was a transitional time for "Joe." He had been depressed for several years, partly because of his parents' divorce. During the school year he had been living in a semi-lockdown Christian boarding school—a place for youth who had not gotten into trouble but were beyond the help of their parents. I thought that if Joe lived with us for the summer, I might be able to reach past the hurt to his heart.

Read the following section silently.

One thing I had neglected to factor in was how Karey's pattern of relating to Joe might differ from mine. I was so focused on winning his heart that I sometimes looked past his behavior, though I drew the line at anything I felt might negatively affect our family. Karey was so focused on his behavior that she found it impossible to form a personal relationship with Joe. Looking back, I think that this unresolved tension taught both Karey and me a lesson—we gravitated to two different approaches. In spite of our differences, we did win his heart, though he continued to struggle with his behavior. Bad habits, addictions, and lack of self-control are much harder to change once a child is grown.

I suspect that what Karey and I experienced that summer might be common. Mothers and fathers have differing roles in the romance. I believe that the most common pattern is for the husband to focus on principles—the big picture or the goal—while the wife tends to focus on down-to-earth details.

Reflection/Discussion

1. What do you think of the conflict Karey and I experienced that summer?

    __ Totally unacceptable for a "Christian" couple (a united front must be maintained at all cost).

    __ Inescapable, considering the situation (it's hard enough to romance your own child).

    __ Adam's fault (my fault—I should have confronted Joe's actions).

    __ Eve's fault (Karey's fault—she should have submitted to my authority).

    __ It was by God's design—it gave Joe a stereoscopic view of God (grace AND justice).

2. If you were to experience a similar conflict in your own parenting, what might be the most constructive resolution?

    __ Withdraw and refuse to discuss it.

    __ Demand your own way.

    __ Blame your spouse.

    __ Send that particular kid to a boarding school.

    __ Acknowledge your differences as a gift from God to your child.

Activity

Tom and Jane have a three-year-old son, Brandon. One day Tom comes home too exhausted to do anything but sit on the loveseat in front of the TV, his arm around Jane. Brandon, on the other hand, has lots of energy. He runs into the dining room, grabs a chair, and drags it to the kitchen—scratching the floor along the way. He climbs onto the counter and opens the cupboard where the cups are kept. As he takes one out, several fall to the floor. On his way back down, Brandon grabs a bag of chocolate chip cookies, but the bag snags and rips, scattering cookies everywhere. Jane is about to intervene, but Tom gently restrains her because he wants to see what their mini-cyclone will do next.

Brandon is already at the refrigerator. He pulls out a full gallon jug of milk, but it is too heavy for him and he drops it. The lid pops off, and suddenly the kitchen floor is swimming in a cookie milk shake.

Next, just as Tom is about to exert his authority to protect his home, Brandon picks a cup out of the mess, pours in some milk, scrapes up some cookie remains from the floor onto a plate, and runs toward his father, saying, "Daddy, I made it for you!"

Unfortunately, the little boy's foot catches on the edge of the carpet right in front of his parents. Brandon does a face plant in Daddy's lap at just about the time the cookies and milk arrive.

Skit:
This skit requires a few props, and a floor that will not be offended by a cookie milk shake. Improvisation is encouraged. For example, fill the jug with rice or beans. To start, have someone narrate this as if it were a script, while three group members play the characters.

What do the parents see? Jane sees an awful mess and a child who needs training. Tom sees a son who loves him enough to bring him cookies and milk when he's tired.

Yes, they will clean up the floor, together. Yes, they will work on Brandon's kitchen skills. But first they will enjoy this rare moment together. Having a clean kitchen is nowhere near as important as reinforcing the compassionate love that made it dirty.

Far more important than what the parents see is what Brandon sees—his parents' stereoscopic love willing to ignore the pervasive messiness of life in favor of the beauty of their little boy's heart.

Read the following silently.

Reflection/Discussion

1. Before sharing, each participant should complete the following sentences.

    As I observed/participated in this skit:

I felt…
I realized…
I wanted…

Have as many group members as wish to comment share their responses. Close with milk and cookies…all around.

PREPARATION FOR SESSION 9:

Read chapter 9, "Profile of a Romancer," in *Romancing Your Child's Heart.*

Personal Task:

Before the next session, review and/or revise your strategy for winning your child's heart in light of what you've learned from this session.

THE PROFILE
OF A ROMANCER

*Children prefer the company of adults
who refuse to take themselves too seriously.*

DAVE BIEBEL

Parents can only expect to infect their children with the desire for God if they are themselves contagious. What our children "catch" from us will have a stronger impact on their hearts than what they are taught in more direct ways. But how do we become contagious?

In Ephesians 5:2 we find a partial answer in the phrase "sweet-smelling aroma." Apostle Paul says that this is what we should be. Something *sweet* is attractive, pleasant, and desired, and *aroma* refers to a distinctive quality that emanates from within—not cheap perfume but the authentic "essence" of romance.

What an unusual earthly phrase to be found in a letter dealing with the spiritual mystery of the church! But then again the church is the bride preparing for the approach of her husband and lover, Christ. This is the nature of Christ's sacrifice and offering to God the Father, and we are to imitate it.

◎ Have someone read
this aloud.

Reflection/Discussion

1. What aromas smell sweet to children?

2. How do parents become a sweet-smelling aroma to their children?

And they said to one another, "Did not our heart burn within us while He talked with us on the road, and while He opened the Scriptures to us?"
(Luke 24:32)

LEADER'S PRAYER: *Father, guide our conversation and brainstorming today, that it would reflect Your heart. And help us as we write our romance strategies. It is so good to have comrades standing with us as we enter this competition for our child's heart.*

In Jesus' name, amen.

SESSION GOAL: To help the participants integrate the following characteristics of a romancer into their strategy for romancing their child's heart:

1. Childlike heart.

2. Everyday hero.

3. Courageous spirit.

4. Joyful heart.

5. Heart of laughter.

6. Glad game spirit.

7. Eye for beauty.

8. Trustworthy heart.

9. Passion for truth.

Brainstorm

One approach to this session is to do a quick brainstorm on each characteristic, recording the material generated (on a white board or something similar) for each family's use as they create their own vision and strategy. During this time your group might be able to add to this list, which was never intended to be exhaustive. If this happens, brainstorm insights related to the additional characteristics as well. After the session, participants may pick and choose from this larger list as they develop their personalized strategy.

Another approach is to choose several objectives and concentrate on them during the session, leaving the rest of the objectives as homework.

Characteristic 1: Childlike heart.

◎ Have someone read this aloud.

Jesus gave His disciples a classic lesson when they were arguing about who should be the greatest in the kingdom. Jesus set a little child before them, to show them the true nature of the kingdom—since they obviously did not understand it. He told them that they could not enter into the kingdom except by becoming like little children—by humbling themselves. This is an infinitely deep truth because it provides insight into the fundamental nature of God.

When children throw themselves creatively, imaginatively, and wholeheartedly into whatever they are doing, they are unself-conscious in the most basic sense—forgetting about themselves. The Greek word for ultimate *self*-consciousness is *hubris,* which means "pride"—putting oneself at the center of the universe. The "childlikeness" Jesus spoke of is the opposite. It is to be hopelessly enthralled, responsive, and open to the possibility that fairy tales are true after all—that there really is a "place beyond time"—a "Brigadoon."

We need to find a way to nurture and nourish the child within us before we can hope to romance the hearts of our children. There is no formula or checklist, no "ten steps to recovery" program. We must simply set the inner child free again. We must remember how to play.

Brainstorm

1. Why is childlikeness so crucial to the romance?

2. Share ways that we as parents can be childlike. Think of words to describe this characteristic of a romancer.

3. Give an example of how it is possible to share experiences with our children in which we are *all* childlike, together.

Characteristic 2: Everyday hero.

Parents are heroes and heroines, larger than life, in their children's eyes. These natural and important roles give children a vision of what they wish to be. When children have this view of their parents, they have hope and strength to dream. A hero/heroine embraces a cause that transcends the value of their own life. This gives all who observe a vision of greater goals and a higher purpose for their lives, as their gaze is lifted from the ground toward the stars, toward God rather than man.

Mothers and fathers complement each other in these roles, as they each communicate different attributes of God's character. A father may portray the brave-hearted image of God the Father, protecting us and taking us on great adventures; a mother may represent the tender, kind-hearted mercy of Christ, who reached out and touched us with unconditional sacrificial love. These images emanate not so much from the actions as from the hearts of mothers and fathers, and color forever their children's perceptions of God.

See Mark 9:33–39 and Matthew 18:1–5.

◎ Have someone read this aloud.

Reflection/Discussion

Share and make a list of examples in your own life where opportunities exist for becoming heroic in your child's eyes.

Characteristic 3: Courageous spirit.

There are tragic chapters in each of our lives that seem antithetic to, but are part of, the Larger Story. The tension of these trials lifts romance to higher and more dazzling heights, in proportion to what is at stake. Without God's grace, the trauma would surely destroy us. Tension demands resolution and produces a climax. Suspense, surprise, hope, courage, heroism, and joy are all connected to our stories. The heroic, courageous suffering of Christ on the cross is the most essential ingredient in the original Love Story. It has an infinite capacity to inspire, as history proves, and to "draw all men" to Him.

To the extent that we trust in the Larger Story and reflect Christ as we face life's tribulations, we also play a role in moving our children's hearts.

Brainstorm

1. Think of the most courageous person you know. What adjectives come to mind?

2. Recall and share a particularly difficult time during which you learned, from watching your parent(s), the deeper meaning of courageous faith.

3. Given similar conditions in your own life, how would you want your children to remember the way you responded?

Characteristic 4: Joyful heart.

At the heart of Christianity is joy—a fruit of the Spirit. It is a gigantic secret that draws us, woos us, and romances us into the company of the cross, which Jesus endured "for the joy set before Him"—our redemption. The journey for a pilgrim can be long, difficult, and exhausting, but when we least expect it, when our hope is nearly extinguished, a turn or a twist surprises us, producing a knowing smile and, soon, laughter. It is an inside joke between us and the One writing the script of the Larger Story. For me it is the last mile along the maple tree–lined country road of my childhood before reaching Grandpa and Grandma's house for Thanksgiving dinner, after a thousand-mile trip when I've been away too long.

As trials and troubles flood our lives our children will seek our eyes. A father in the LMCC class said that one of the best evidences of joy in this situation is a smile and a "knowing" wink given to a child. Such a simple act, but so powerful for our children.

Brainstorm

How can we express joy to our children?

Characteristic 5: Heart of laughter.

If you are like me, you are far more attracted to someone who can laugh than to someone who is as serious as death all the time. We are drawn to this type of Christian because they seem to have a special, personal, intimate connection with God. One of my friends makes me laugh, but sometimes after the fact I can't recall what was so funny.

 Have several group members tell jokes, then have someone read the following aloud.

On one occasion, for example, we were out to dinner and he kept us laughing for nearly two hours, until I started getting cheek cramps. The strange thing was, after we left the restaurant, I couldn't recall a single "joke." It was more a sense of lightheartedness, marked by wit with some wisdom thrown in besides, that made our night so enjoyable—plus the fact that this particular person has all the reason in the world to be bitter instead of funny. He can still smile and laugh even though the world around him has crumbled and Christian friends have deserted him, because he clings to the hope that the Larger Story is true. This is why I consider him one of the most heroic men I know.

Brainstorm

Think of practical ways to laugh a lot, and to even schedule laughter into your parenting.

Characteristic 6: Glad game spirit.

We've already looked at the glad game, which is the central theme of the book *Pollyanna*. This game is really quite simple. When something happens that doesn't line up with our wishes or expectations, we look for anything in it that we might be glad about. The more difficult it is to find the glad thing, the more exciting and challenging is the game. Kids play this game naturally, but it seems harder for adults. I suspect this is because children are more optimistic than adults—hope runs through their lives like a silver thread, drawing then naturally into the glad game.

Have someone read this aloud.

When we play the glad game, we look for evidence of the Larger Story in what might otherwise be a difficult situation. I know of a large family in which this process is a private joke. The key phrase is, "Oh, wow!"

"Wow" backwards is still "wow." So, no matter what life throws our way, we can still find the WOW in it.

Brainstorm

Think of situations and circumstances where the glad game would work, drawing your child into the Larger Story.

Characteristic 7: Eye for beauty.

 Have someone read this aloud.

Once, Dawson and I were camping at ten thousand feet. One afternoon I realized he had not been in camp for several hours so I hiked up the ridge looking for him. I found him sitting on a ledge gazing out on the valley and cliffs thousands of feet below. At first I wondered what in the world he was looking at. Then I saw the white new snow on the red rock framed by gold aspen quaking in the bright sunny blue of the September sky. It took my breath away. No wonder Dawson had sat there for hours.

The power of beauty can make us uncomfortable, to the point of writing it off as earthly or dangerously trivial, for Satan has counterfeited beauty and all but monopolized it for his own purposes. We must reclaim this tool of romance by exposing our children to the beauty of creation and the beauty in the world of human creations inspired by God. This process should involve searching for it and bringing it into our homes and lives—on purpose. We must aggressively enter the beauty contest for our child's heart.

Brainstorm

List ways parents can use beauty to win their child's heart. Organize the list by the age of the child.

Characteristic 8: Trustworthy heart.

 Have someone read this aloud.

A surefire way to destroy the hope that children naturally have is to break promises. Sadly, by the time they reach third grade most children have lost their childlike trust. Once Teddy Roosevelt was entertaining visiting statesmen when he exclaimed, "I must ask you to excuse me. We'll finish this talk some other time. I promised the boys I'd go shooting with them at four o'clock and I never keep boys waiting. It's a hard trial for a boy to wait."

My friend Kathy once said, "God doesn't tease. He's not like that." She wasn't referring to ordinary play, but to someone with power playing with someone vulnerable, as a cat plays with a mouse. Trust is incompatible with abusive teasing. Parents often get away with such behavior because children are resilient and responsive, and they forgive easily. But they have their limits, and eventually they do suffer damage—to their emotions, their spirits, their view of the world, and most importantly to their ability to trust God. A parent's trustworthiness will place either solid ground or quicksand under their child's feet.

In your journal, answer: Do my children trust me?

Brainstorm

What makes a parent trustworthy?

Characteristic 9: Passion for truth.

 Have someone read this aloud.

Our home has nine libraries and many filing cabinets filled with notes, data, and papers we have gathered over the years. Karey and I love the journey along the way of wisdom—taking experiences, information, and knowledge to a philosophical level, and putting the puzzle together in the context of a Christian worldview. We collect truth, file it, save it, and synthesize it—like Sherlock Holmes and Watson on the trail of a mystery, or archeologists discussing the results of a dig. It is no small thing when our children witness this. I know our curiosity is contagious, for they all have begun their own search for truth.

Karey and I often wake up with fascinating ideas from our bedtime reading, carrying them to the breakfast table and beyond. Sometimes our kids raise their eyebrows at each other, wondering what in the world we are talking about. It's exciting to think of all there is to learn, observe, and contemplate for the rest of our lives.

Proverbs compares the way of wisdom to a treasure hunt for God's truth and its application to life, the discovery of which brings great pleasure.

Brainstorm

How do you search for God's truth?

CONCLUSION: Close with group prayer asking the Lord to show you creative ways to take your family in the direction you sense He would like you to go.

PREPARATION FOR SESSION 10:

1. Read chapter 10, "Methods for Romancers," in *Romancing Your Child's Heart*.

2. Bring your favorite photo album to session 10.

3. If you engage in a craft that uses special tools, bring a finished example of your work to show, and one or more unique tools to describe to the group.

4. Return to your "strategy" for romancing your child's heart, plugging in the insights you have gained about the profile of a romancer, and asking the Lord for grace to develop any that may be lacking.

Group Leader: Bring a book of children's fairy tales to session 10. If any group members are craftsmen or craftswomen, encourage them to bring unique tools and samples of their work to session 10. Be sure that the props and/or supplies needed for activities in session 10 are available.

JOURNALING TOPICS:

1. Tell your life's story by starting out: "Once upon a time, there was...."

2. What part(s) of your story do your children not know yet that you should tell them? There is the temptation to "brag" about our mistakes and sins and even use our children as therapists. Discretion and common sense are in order here so we don't lead our children astray.

WIELDING THE TOOLS OF ROMANCE

A bow, like a violin, is a work of art....
Every good bow is a work of love....
A true archer must be a craftsman.

SAXTON POPE

Saxton Pope was one of the most famous archers since Robin Hood. Using Pope's book as a guide, Dawson and I sculpted a longbow from a seasoned stave of Missouri Osage that had once been a fencepost. This golden orange wood is considered the best for making longbows, because of its straight grain and resilience. Our challenge was to follow the grain God created in the wood to release the bow that already existed within. Our goal was to "romance" the bow out of the wood. This required vision, patience, and skill, as well as special hand tools: a drawknife, bench vise, spokeshave, jack plane, and calipers. The tools were essential for us to produce a bow with proper proportions, tiller, symmetry, and arc—one that would brilliantly cast an arrow along the right trajectory.

So it is with romancing a child's heart. The methods of romance are the tools. As in crafting a bow, the key is the skill with which we wield these tools.

LEADER'S PRAYER: *Father, guide our conversation and brainstorming today so that they will reflect Your heart. Help us understand the methods for romancers so we can integrate then into our strategies.*
In Jesus' name, Amen.

Show-and-Tell: Group members who are craftsmen or craftswomen—and who use special tools—mechanics, furniture makers, weavers, and so forth—should explain or demonstrate how several of these tools are used.

◎ Have someone read this aloud.

Greater love has no one than this, than to lay down one's life for his friends.
(John 15:13)

Note:
As with session 9, if you don't finish the entire session during your allotted time, you can always come back to it later on your own.

◎ Have someone read this aloud.

Ephesians 5:15

SESSION GOAL: To encourage the participants to integrate the following methods of a romancer into their strategy for romancing their child's heart.

Methods

1. Use ordinary opportunities.

2. Tell stories.

3. Establish family traditions.

4. Share unique experiences.

5. Allow freedom at home.

6. Become a kindred spirit.

7. Be willing to sacrifice.

8. Encourage a good path.

9. Help the helpless.

Method 1: Use ordinary opportunities.

In the book, I talk about going to the hardware store, but instead of going alone, I take Travis with me and use this joint activity as a tool for romancing. Sadly, for every little boy or girl in our world whose father might do this, there is a father or mother who is too often so focused on achieving life's little goals that he or she fails to see the opportunities to make their child prince or princess for an hour or a day—and so accomplish an eternal work in their hearts. Our noble missions, which even include legitimate ministry involvements, steal time that ought to be given to our children.

If we are wise parents we will make the most of every opportunity, because the days are evil. The evil one will steal away opportunities if we let him. Even interruptions can be opportunities. If our children irritate us and we ignore them, we may be missing the best blessings in life. They may have more to do with God's plans than with ours.

Brainstorm

Make a list of ordinary opportunities we tend to overlook that have great potential for connecting with our child's heart.

Method 2: Tell stories.

A newspaper article once included children's answers to the question: "What would happen if there were no stories in the world?" One child said, "People would die of seriousness." Another said, "When you went to bed at night it would be boring, because your head would be blank."

Most people are natural storytellers. As we sit around a dinner table, fireplace, or campfire, or share a cup of coffee with a friend, stories roll off our lips—about our families, our friendships, our lives. We have only a finite number of days with our children. Once we grasp the importance of storytelling as a tool in the romance of our child's heart, we will realize that we need to begin at once. We can all be effective, especially if the stories are from our own experiences.

One of the greatest benefits of hospitality is that guests bring the world to our table through their stories. Our own children, as they grew, lingered longer and longer around the table. They would leave and then come back, and eventually they would stay. Many times we have been spellbound, or we laughed so hard we literally cried, as we listened to our guests' stories.

Brainstorm

List storytelling opportunities and ways to stimulate participation.

Method 3: Establish family traditions.

Our greatest challenge in romancing our child's heart is to continually live in the Larger Story. The spiritual discipline of celebration, expressed in family traditions, is designed to help us do just that. Celebrations remind us of God in our midst. They give perspective and lift our eyes to the Larger Story.

The word "holiday" comes from "holy day"—a special day that was set apart for a spiritual purpose. The primary purpose of such times was to point to the Larger Story through celebration and feasting, usually around the family table. Praise of God was the focus, not out of duty or obligation but out of joy. As children participate through our traditions in the dramatization, they enter the story. This is not some make-believe play—it is reality for a Christian, because it connects us to eternity past and brings God's mighty works throughout creation and history into our lives.

Traditions we do for our children alone are not as attractive to our children as traditions we do for ourselves while also including them. When we are personally engaged, the tradition becomes much more genuine and builds feelings of security in a child. Traditions communicate to our children that we all belong to something bigger—something of deeper significance than stories about Santa Claus or the Easter bunny. Our shared experiences will draw them in, captivating their affections, romancing them to God.

◎ Have someone read this aloud.

◎ Have someone read this aloud.

I inherited several family traditions from my childhood, and Karey and I have created some of our own. For example, the first present we open is the family Bible. Our latest addition is our "third day of Christmas" smorgasbord—a whole day dedicated to ethnic foods and fellowship—reflecting on our human heritage and contemplating how God has worked through it. We invite close friends of different heritages to share their histories. We exchange stories about God's hand in our lives. Times like these around our dining room table are times of authentic fellowship, offering a glimpse of heaven.

Brainstorm

1. Describe, from your childhood, your favorite family tradition.

2. What traditions do you celebrate (or would you like to celebrate) as a family?

Method 4: Share unique experiences.

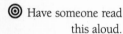 Have someone read this aloud.

The lifeblood of friendship is shared experiences. Facts and belief do not connect hearts the way sharing an experience does. The more unique and unusual the shared experience, the stronger the relationship becomes. Traumatic, challenging, exhilarating, exhausting, frightening, and mysterious experiences are the ones we remember best— they are vivid in our memory. Orchestrating unique experiences with our children connects our hearts.

One father suggested that parents sit down and plan twelve "cool" things to do with their kids. For example, you might surprise your children tonight by pitching a blanket tent in the living room, inviting them to crawl under so you could read a story by candle-light. Or instead of watching TV, you might pop popcorn and then take a blanket and your child outside and lie on your backs and watch the universe. Better yet, bring a couple of pillows and spend the night under the stars with your child.

Brainstorm

1. Create a list of unique experiences that have the potential to deepen and strengthen your relationship with your child.

2. From your favorite photo album, select one photo or series of photos from the same experience, and share what makes this particular memory unique.

3. As a group, see if you can identify a common theme (or themes) that underlie(s) the uniqueness of all the memories selected.

Method 5: Allow freedom at home.

My mother met the challenge of keeping house for four very athletic sons with her usual artistic panache. She reasoned that we were programmed to be physical, and to fight or try to control this innate tendency would frustrate us, distract us from our schoolwork, and create unnecessary stress for everyone. So with Dad's help, Mom boy-proofed the house and saved her valuable antiques. They bought two sturdy four-legged end tables and two brass lamps. They threaded the lamp cords through holes drilled in the tabletops and bolted down the lamps. Of course, when we bumped a lamp the table and lamp fell over, but it was easy to set it up again because it was in one piece.

Our boy-proofed house still had unmovable boundaries that our parents set for us. Mom's antique curved-glass china cabinet was symbolic of one of those boundaries. It was left in the house, filled with delicate dishes, vases, and bowls, many of them from Sweden. By God's grace, that cabinet was never touched, even when my youngest brother convinced Mom that it was essential for him to practice dribbling his basketball indoors.

The bottom line in such matters depends upon our highest objective as parents. A mother once told me, as she reflected on raising several sons, "If I had it to do over again, I wouldn't spend as much time cleaning the stove. I would spend that time with my boys. The stove is long gone and nobody really cares anymore, including me, how clean it was. But my boys—they are the treasure of my life."

Brainstorm

1. As you hear how my parents boy-proofed our home, what thoughts cross your mind?

   __ They were too lenient.
   __ Basketball in my house is out of the question.
   __ My motto is: Dirty house = dirty life.
   __ Their priorities were right: people first, then things.
   __ Other: _____.

2. If you were teaching your child to ride a bike, you would naturally choose a flat, smooth surface and clear it of obstacles until the child has become skilled enough to avoid the obstacles and negotiate hills and curves. How does this idea apply to providing an atmosphere of freedom in your home? List ways in which you could make your home more conducive to romancing your child's heart?

 Have someone read this aloud.

Method 6: Become a kindred spirit.

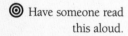 Have someone read this aloud.

"Kindred spirit" is a fascinating concept. "Kin" means related and "ship" means a quality or state of being. Thus it is a dynamic relationship based on something beyond just us. As Christians, we are "kin" with the Holy Spirit and enjoy the ultimate kinship. This is a deep spiritual truth that is manifested with a child in ordinary, seemingly earthly ways.

For example, my brother Scott has sons who excel in the all-American sports of basketball, football, and baseball...all of which he loves. However, when one son took a liking to soccer, which Scott never played, and for which he had little affinity, he said without hesitation, "If my son likes soccer, then I like soccer."

Kathy, a close friend of ours, is mother to eleven children. It takes ingenuity and insight to connect personally with each child, and she shared with me that sometimes the most obvious way is to look into their eyes. Eyes truly are the windows to the soul—they reveal the heart, and a child will know by our eyes that we can be trusted. Kathy and her youngest son have a morning "gazing time," when she looks deeply into his eyes with a lingering look of fondness, humor, and enjoyment. She has done this with all of her children since they were babies. She tries to catch each of her children's eyes when they approach, to let them know, uniquely, that they are the one she loves and wants to know.

Brainstorm

1. As a group, brainstorm all the words that come to mind when you think of the term "kindred spirit."

2. In your journal, write all that you think would be valuable in romancing your child.

3. Discuss which of these qualities are natural and which can be developed with practice?

Method 7: Be willing to sacrifice.

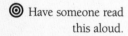 Have someone read this aloud.

One thing my parents did to win my heart was to allow me to pick out our new family car when I was in junior high. I'll never forget that ivory-colored 1963 Dodge slant-six. My criteria for choosing it were sleek looks, sleek looks, sleek looks—so I get no credit for the fact that it was the best car we ever owned. I used it in college, as did one of my brothers, and we drove it well over a hundred thousand miles.

Allowing me this much freedom came so naturally to Mom and Dad that today they hardly recall it. *But I do.* And it means as much to me today as it did then. They wooed my heart by listening to me, believing in me, trusting me, and then following through by putting their money—literal, hard-earned cash—where their respect was.

Reflection/Discussion

1. My parents' sacrifice for us is symbolized by memories of a car. Reflect on the price your parents paid to raise you, and describe any symbols that come to mind.

2. Projecting yourself beyond the end of your own child-rearing years, what symbols of the price you're paying now would you want your child(ren) to remember?

Method 8: Encourage a good path.

My wife Karey wrote in her book *Hearth and Home*:

> My desire [was] to inspire and guide my children's higher instincts and convictions.... As they chose good, I'd praise. We gave much praise when they took their first steps, said their first words, learned to use the toilet, tied their shoes, and rode a bike. As they [got] older...we decided to acknowledge and continue focusing on the good skills, behaviors, and attitudes. We almost ignored the bad behavior. I said *almost*. (I don't mean "bad" as in the sense of disobeying laws of nature and God's absolutes.)[2]

Encouraging a good path is a simple but powerful parenting method. Instead of always harping on your children's faults, tell them of their virtues. A healthy balance is fifteen praises to one criticism.

◎ Have someone read this aloud.

Brainstorm

1. Estimate your praise/criticism ratio. Circle the ratio that most closely matches: 15/1; 10/1; 5/1; 1/1; 1/5; 1/10; 1/15.

2. Which way do you want to move?

3. What dangers do you see in going too far to the left or right?

4. List examples of encouraging a good path.

◎ Have someone read
this aloud.

If a child lives with praise,
He learns to appreciate.
If a child lives with fairness,
He learns justice.
If a child lives with security,
He learns to have faith.

If a child lives with approval,
He learns to like himself.
If a child lives with acceptance and friendship,
He learns to find love in the world.
—DOROTHY LAW NOLTE

Method 9: Help the helpless.

Once Travis traveled to Mexico and helped build a house for a family. In an essay describing this experience he wrote:

> Sitting on the motel bed eating pizza, I started thinking about little Julio, and I felt ashamed. My primary thought since the storm had been washing a little dirty water off my leg. Julio's house was so flimsy. If that storm had blown my tent down, what had it done to his house? Was he still out there wrapped in plastic and shivering in the rain? Did the flood carry him away? I suddenly lost my appetite for the pizza in my hand. I quietly put it back in the delivery box and walked out into the rain.
>
> I began to understand now why I had taken this trip. I thought about how many other Julios there were out in the storm, and all over the world. I realized that this problem is too big for me. I became angry and then frustrated. Soon I sank into a helpless despair. All the things that I have filled my life with seem trivial compared to the needs of Julio. As the rain stopped, my emotions calmed. Then like the night sky that had cleared, my mind cleared itself of the confusing thoughts that had filled it. I realized that I cannot change the world by myself, but while I was in Mexico, I helped change the world for one child and his family.

James 1:27 says, "Pure and undefiled religion before God and the Father is this: to visit orphans and widows in their trouble."

"Orphans and widows" can be considered a metaphor for the helpless. In Luke 14:13–14, Jesus says, "When you give a feast, invite the poor, the maimed, the lame, the blind. And you will be blessed, because they cannot repay you."

Brainstorm

1. Why does the act of helping the helpless affect the heart so powerfully?

2. List ways that you can help your children be involved in helping someone who can not repay them.

Ponder

Of all the methods for romancing covered in this session and/or the book, which one do you feel you most need the Lord's help in wielding effectively?

Pray

Allow all who wish to share to name this need, and then pray, around the group, for each other.

AFTER THE SESSION:

Return to your strategy for romancing your child's heart, integrating insights you have gained about methods for romancers. Pray for the needs expressed at the end of session 10.

PREPARATION FOR SESSION 11:

1. Read chapter 11, "The Sense of Wonder," in *Romancing Your Child's Heart*.

2. Prepare a sample unit study (see session 11, objective 3) if you volunteered to do so.

Note:
Before completing this session, please look ahead to the activities suggested for session 11, objective 3. Your group leader needs volunteers for either or both of the upcoming unit studies.

Group Leader:
As appropriate, remind your volunteers [session 11, objective 3] to bring their unit studies to the meeting.

———

PROTECTING THE SENSE OF WONDER

Wine from water is not so small.
But an even better magic trick is that anything is here at all.
So the challenging thing becomes not to look for miracles,
But find where there isn't one.

LYRICS FROM "HOLY NOW," BY PETER MAYER

Near the end of a conference, I wandered over to a window. The verdant green of a well-tended soccer field stretched out before me in the summer sun. Gazing at the restful scene, I noticed a mud puddle near the sidelines. A little boy sat in the middle, wiggling his barely visible toes in the chocolate water. Applying some secret logic that only little boys can understand, his shoes and socks lay at the edge of the pool, completely clean and dry, while the rest of his clothes were being soaked.

After a while, I realized that a woman was standing beside me, watching the boy, too. I assumed she was his mother, but no hint of disapproval or reprimand clouded her face.

I turned and asked, "Who taught you how to romance your son's heart like this?"

She remained quiet for several moments, gazing out the window. As my question lingered in the air and seemed to wither, several thoughts ran through my mind:

1. She is embarrassed because of his childlike behavior.

2. She is afraid of the germs lurking in the chocolate water.

3. She is theologically illiterate in this area.

◎ Have someone read this aloud.

When she responded, it was as if I had asked the most natural question in the world.

"Ever since his little brother died from leukemia last year, I see things differently. I have learned the difference between things that matter and those that are incidental. He is with me and we love each other—that matters. A little dirt and water don't. He is just a little boy loving God's creation in a way that makes God smile—in a state of innocent wonder. Who am I to rob them both of this pleasure?"

A temporal perspective would see dirt, germs, and inconvenience. This wise woman's viewpoint tells the Larger Story—that eternity intersects time when a little boy wonders that his toes can wiggle even when he can't see his legs. From an eternal perspective, we see a child's fascination, curiosity, amazement, and breathless enchantment at a creation with God's fingerprints and brush strokes all over it.

With all that at stake, why would we rush to extricate our children from muddy puddles?

Reflection/Discussion

1. What would be your most likely response to your first sight of your young child sitting in a mud puddle, wiggling his or her toes?

2. What other options can you imagine?

LEADER'S PRAYER: *Father, as adults we have all to some degree lost our sense of wonder and overlooked the miracle of Creation. Open our eyes to again see, as we saw as children, the mystery, beauty, and story in the world around us. For then we will be ready to enter this important arena of romance.*
    In Jesus' name we pray, amen.

SESSION GOAL: **To prepare participants to help their child get to know the Creator through His creation, by developing their own personal strategy to protect and cultivate their child's sense of wonder.**

SESSION OBJECTIVES

1. To develop a plan for protecting your child's sense of wonder.

2. To develop a "curriculum" through which to cultivate your child's sense of wonder.

3. To plan one unit study designed around your child's area(s) of interest.

When I consider Your heavens, the work of Your fingers, the moon and the stars, which You have ordained, what is man that You are mindful of him, and the son of man that You visit him? (Psalm 8:3–4)

Objective 1: To develop a plan for protecting your child's sense of wonder.

Children are spontaneously and naturally drawn to things that make them wonder, especially God's creation. Because children naturally live in the present, they savor the moment and the sheer sensory experience. Perhaps this is why Christ spoke of the ideal of childlikeness. When children wonder at the world around them, they may be the closest of all people to comprehending the reality of God. Often this is expressed by a wide-open mouth. They believe in story—in the sky, in the rocks, in the water, in the trees, and in the animals. This captivates them, draws them, and romances their hearts.

⊚ Have someone read this aloud.

For many of us, the most vivid memories we have from childhood involve nature. Nature's stories wooed and romanced us to God, even if we had not been taught about Him and it was only an indefinable longing. Our natural awareness grew, fueled by the fascination we had for God's handiwork.

Sadly, children wonder naturally but adults soon teach them to end this esoteric pursuit. Most children's sense of wonder is crushed or lost by the time they reach third grade, through a secular culture that brings futile and cynical despondency into their once wonder-filled lives. Adult Christians can also discourage this wide-mouthed wonder; for example, by systematically providing all the "answers" without listening to what the child's questions may be.

Either way, by the time most children have become adults, they will have fallen into routines, grown complacent, adopting more or less pragmatic lives. As they've gotten "bigger," everything else has grown smaller. Words like *blasé, worldly wise* and *sophisticated* describe grown-ups who have become adultish, and have stopped asking "silly" childlike questions.

Reflection/Discussion

1. Recall and share an experience you had as a child that left you wide-mouthed in wonder.

2. Brainstorm a list of ways to protect your children's sense of wonder.

Objective 2: To develop a "curriculum" through which to cultivate your child's sense of wonder.

We can feed our children's sense of wonder through a systematic, hands-on exploration of the earth. Children who touch rocks, catch butterflies, and watch clouds become naturalists in the whimsical sense, whether they choose science as a vocation, hobby, or simply as a vehicle to deeper worship of God the Creator. Children need to see, smell, hear, touch, and taste God's creation. Our goal is experience, not analysis. Unless children ask for facts

⊚ Have someone read this aloud.

about what they are experiencing, these are not the times for scientific lectures. Our primary role is to participate in a childlike way by engaging our own five senses—and our heart—in a shared, uncomplicated experience. Participation with a child in the activity of wonder will romance that child's heart...if we avoid sermonizing.

As an earth scientist, I recommend a curriculum organized around the spheres of the earth. The activities suggested in the book, and many more like them, bring parents and children together into direct contact with nature. As we cultivate our child's sense of wonder, our own sense of wonder will be stimulated, too. We will become like children, enjoying again those things that the responsibilities of adulthood have crowded out of our lives.

Brainstorm

1. On a white board or chalkboard have someone create five columns, one for each sphere of the earth—atmosphere (air), hydrosphere (water), lithosphere (crust), biosphere (life), and athenosphere (mantle). List in each column ideas for activities that will bring you and your child into direct contact with that sphere.

2. In your journal plan to do these by scheduling them into your life. Make appropriate notes on your calendar.

Objective 3: To plan one unit study designed around your child's area(s) of interest.

Unit study can come in a variety of shapes and sizes—the best being delight-driven, because these flow from our child's natural inclinations and curiosities. When children's passions are ignited by some interest, then the study is personalized. They own it and end up investing much more energy in the study than they otherwise might. Unit studies can be called special projects, hobbies, extracurricular activities, research, or play.

One spring we began a project called "The Flowers of Evergreen." Our family decided that, instead of just casually looking at the flowers in our meadow, we would study them, photograph them, smell them—get to know them firsthand. This experience was like examining the brush strokes of a master Artist, who painted our meadow with delicate, extravagantly beautiful flowers—some of which bloomed for just a few days until, to paraphrase the psalmist, the Chinook winds blew and they were gone and their place remembered them no more.

But we remembered them—more than two hundred in all. Our study began when Travis (eight at the time) informed us that a purple pasqueflower had pushed its way up

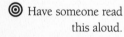
See the book for review, if you need more detail.

Have someone read this aloud.

Psalm 103:15

through the melting snow. I grabbed my camera, Karey, and Heather, and brought along several flower guidebooks and a notebook. We then followed Travis through scattered snowdrifts to the first flower of the year. The study ended with the first September frost.

We photographed, sketched, and dried flowers. We carefully cataloged the whole thing, then organized it into a slide show, which we presented to grandparents, friends, and local community groups.

Activity

Unit Studies: Consider one or both of the suggested "unit studies" below, brought to the session by volunteers (we hope!) from the group. If no one brings any materials, discuss hobbies that group members may have, sharing the background of each person's interest in his/her hobby, and what it takes to pursue it.

1. A show-and-tell hobby (e.g., collecting rocks or butterflies, pressing wild-flowers—activities a child could do with an adult). Have the volunteer tell how and when his/her passion for this subject developed, and what is necessary to pursue a similar project.

2. A unit study on herbs, vegetables, or flowers found in a local grocery store—an example of activity that could be done anywhere by anyone. The volunteer should have obtained samples and found out all he or she could discover about the subject matter, organizing the material into an outline and bringing the items studied to class.

Brainstorm

As a group, brainstorm all the "unit studies" you can think of to do with your children, considering your setting, available time, resources, interests, and expertise.

Personalize

As individual parent(s), select from this list all unit studies that you believe might match your child's interests.

Remember: Each child is unique.

Then, from this shorter list, select one to three unit studies that you could launch in the near future, and integrate these into the action plan of your personalized strategy.

Don't forget that once you've settled on some potential unit studies, you should run your ideas past your child to see which projects ignite his or her sense of wonder.

I will never forget the response of our youngest, Dawson, when I suggested that we do a wildflower study like the one his brother and sister had done.

"No, thanks," he said. "I've already started my own study."

"But you don't understand," I argued. "We will learn all about edible plants, and we can collect specimens."

"Papa, I know all about the study Heather and Travis did," Dawson replied, "but I want to do one on bugs." Today the main attraction for guests in the Swan home is Dawson's insect collection.

CONCLUDE THE SESSION WITH THE LEADER READING THE FOLLOWING, THEN CLOSING IN PRAYER.

We as parents have the responsibility and privilege to protect and cultivate our children's sense of wonder. Fortunately, God has made this easy through the beauty and intricacy of His creation. Our role is to provide the opportunity for them to experience and explore it—and to share these endeavors with them as fellow treasure hunters (sometimes called "scientists"). God will do the rest—for us, and in us.

> With a quiver of arrows, a dog at his side,
> The sun on his shoulders, a gleam in his eye,
> The whimsical wisdom he shares with me,
> Paints a picture of life, it's somethin' to see.
>
> He builds forts in the trees and forts underground,
> And some out of old aspen logs.
> His goal's in the making, the building, creating,
> And not in what's finished and done.
>
> And when the fires of his wonder warm my soul,
> His honest brown eyes let me know.
> I'll hold this moment as long as I can,
> For it may never come 'round again.

LYRICS FROM "FIRES OF HIS WONDER,"
BY MONTE SWAN

Preparation for Session 12:

1. Read chapter 12, "The Creative Image," and chapter 13, "Creative Domains," in *Romancing Your Child's Heart.*

2. Continue refining your personal strategy, with the goal of having its first draft done by the end of session 12.

Extra Credit

The next time your child "sits in a mud puddle," walk up to him, take off your shoes and socks (remembering to place them high and dry next to the chocolate water), step up to the edge of the puddle, plant your feet shoulder's width apart, and jump in. It will be worth it just seeing the expression on your child's face.

Group Leader: Skim session 12 and bring to the session the props needed for the activities.

DISCOVERING THE CREATIVE IMAGE

Every night after supper, our front yard was our stage
With an evening sky...and the smell of sage.

LYRICS FROM "FAMILY COUNTRY YARD," BY DEBBIE MAURELLO

There is a place, an enchanted place, down near our spring, cradled by a granite ledge where an aspen grove meets a stand of giant blue spruce and Douglas fir. In this secluded meadow, edged with a raspberry patch and carpeted with purple violets, we found the name for our home—Singing Springs. Often I have dreamed of building a log cabin there, with a porch for sitting and songwriting, for creating and contemplating. I have put it off partly because I have so many projects underway, but also partly because I did not want to disturb the pristine beauty God placed there. Yet every time I walk down the path that takes me to the forest beyond, I design and construct this cabin in my imagination.

So when I heard about the newest fort that Dawson was building "down by the spring," I went to investigate.

The most beautiful part of my little meadow was a big mess. Scrap lumber, even particleboard, had been dragged in from some construction site and was strewn about, crushing the tender spring grass and wildflowers. The beginning of a frame was taking shape. The design was "pole barn, circa 1970." It was not square or level. Sixteen-penny nails, painstakingly driven, held it together. The shock and disgust froze my heart with anger.

◎ Have someone read this aloud.

Stop and Discuss

1. If you were me, what would you do next? (Check all that apply.)

__ Yell at Dawson for doing something like this without asking.

__ Make him clean up the mess and restore the beauty.

__ Make him tear down his "fort."

__ Establish limits and guidelines so he wouldn't do such a thing again.

__ Other: _____.

2. What might inspire a ten-year-old to tackle such a project?

3. Is this characteristic common in children? If so, what is its source?

◎ Have someone read this aloud.

After a few seconds passed, something struck my heart and the ice melted as the reality of my little boy's passion swept over me like a sweet storm. He had begun construction with the best materials he could find, following his own original design. He had placed it not just anywhere in my meadow but in *the best spot* in my meadow—the spot that even the designs in my imagination refused to consider because of its sacredness.

As the fires of his wonder warmed my soul, tears welled in my eyes and it dawned on me—this is the creative image of God incarnate in my little boy! He had made this pristine place a holy place. I joined in God's joy, and smiled and smiled and smiled.

Reflection/Discussion

1. Ponder the contrast between the perspectives in this true story. Describe the spiritual difference.

2. Why is it so devastating to a child when the threat to his/her creative image comes from his/her parents?

3. Why are parents typically unaware that they are damaging the creative image of God in their child?

Dateline: Evergreen, Colorado—June 2002.

Sequel to the "Dawson's fort in my pristine meadow" saga— to be read aloud.

Dawson's youth pastor called to ask a favor. Because of the extreme forest fire danger that summer, the national forest where he had planned to take the group camping had been closed. "I was wondering," he said, "if we could camp out in your meadow, the one down by a spring Dawson has told me about."

"Sure," I replied, wondering if God was playing a joke on me. "When will you need it?"

"In about two hours," he said.

"How long will you need it?"

"Four days."

"How many kids?"

"Forty-five." He paused. "We'll get some portapotties."

During those four days I witnessed more "fort building" by boys than I had ever seen. The girls? Well, they pitched their tents in a circle right in the middle of my pristine meadow—though they were relatively kind to the flora as they engaged in the eternally important activity of community.

> **LEADER'S PRAYER:** *Father, help us comprehend the significance and power of Your creative image expressed in our child. Help us discover, protect, and cultivate it. As we develop a specific plan, lead us to the unique areas of creativity You have prepared for our children.*
> *In Jesus' name, amen.*

SESSION GOAL: **To help participants develop their own personal strategies to protect and cultivate the creative image of God in their child, and discover and develop their child's creative domains.**

SESSION OBJECTIVES

1. To develop a plan for protecting the creative image of God in your child.

2. To develop a plan (a vision) to create an atmosphere in your home and most of all in your heart that will encourage and inspire uninhibited healthy creativity in your child.

3. To develop a plan to provide long uninterrupted stretches of time and proper materials and tools for creative play.

4. To develop a plan to discover your child's creative domain(s).

5. To formulate a plan to develop your child's creative domain(s).

Objective 1: *To develop a plan for protecting the creative image of God in your child.*

Within us all dwells the potential to create according to the uniqueness God gave us. To be creative is to have the ability to bring into existence, to cause, or to make. This power is expressed in designing, inventing, shaping, and organizing through imaginative skill and ingenuity—an innate ability in humans, transmitted to us from God. The mere fact that we

In the beginning God created the heavens and the earth. (Genesis 1:1)

So God created man in His own image; in the image of God He created him. (Genesis 1:27)

You may not be able to complete the discussion of all these objectives in your allotted time. The group may choose to focus on several, instead of all of them, or to quickly brainstorm the entire list.

◎ Have someone read this aloud.

can create at all is evidence that there is a divine blueprint, not only for each of us personally, but for all humanity.

The creative image of God in us demands expression. When we create, we comprehend God better—even feel a holy camaraderie with Him. We own the process. This is a powerful reality. Children long for this ownership when they say the revealing words, "Let *me* do it."

Resources: Saving Childhood *by the Medveds;* The Hurried Child *by David Elkind;* Endangered Minds *by Jane Healy;* Children Without Childhood *by Marie Winn; and* The Disappearance of Childhood *by Neil Postman.*

If our children's creativity points them to God, revealing Him as its source, it will play an important role in the romance of their hearts. But if they grow up entertained by cartoon characters, superheroes, videotapes, video games, toys, electronic gadgets, and amusements, our children will become creatively constipated, their minds and hearts stagnant receptacles instead of fountains of creative energy bringing joy to themselves and to those around them.

Brainstorm

1. List areas of danger (or threats) to the creative image in your child(ren).

2. How can these dangers be thwarted—in other words, how can your child(ren)'s creative image be protected?

Objective 2: To develop a plan (a vision) to create an atmosphere in your home and most of all in your heart that will encourage and inspire uninhibited healthy creativity in your child.

Have someone read this aloud.

When Dawson was four years old, he built a fort out of pillows in our parlor. At the end of the day, Karey went to help him put the pillows back in their proper places. She reached down to pick up the first pillow and it would not move. She tried another—and then another. They were all nailed through the carpet into the subfloor!

Tell the person next to you how you would respond if your four-year-old did this. Then continue reading aloud.

Karey just stood there in amazement—and then laughed and even praised Dawson for his creativity (of course making sure that he understood this was not at all good for the pillows or the carpet). He has never done it again. She often shudders as she imagines how she would have reacted had this happened when our older children were young, when she was less experienced and knowledgeable about a child's creativity, spirit, defiance, and will. A parent must make some difficult judgments, but I would rather err on the side of grace, by interpreting such actions as childishness. I would rather overprotect than underprotect their creative spirits.

Perhaps the greatest gift we can give our children, to protect and nurture the creative image of God in them, is the freedom to be themselves—uninhibited and unafraid to create, to imagine, to feel, and then to find God's calling for their lives. The atmosphere in a home originates in the hearts of the parents. When children are secure in knowing we will not ridicule or reject them, but will accept them for who they are, the creative image in them flourishes. When we treasure their creativity and their creations, we bring them not only joy, but also the confidence and freedom to discover the expression of God's creative image in them.

Creating this kind of environment takes time, energy, and willingness to invest our resources. It also requires commitment to the process of romancing our child's heart to the One who is the source of all creative endeavors.

Activity

1. Rate your home atmosphere in terms of its creativity quotient (percent) by placing a check mark on the scale below:

Sterile   Neutral   Fertile

0_____50_____100%

2. Now draw a hammer and nail over the point where you'd like to be one year from now.

3. Brainstorm a plan to redesign your home atmosphere so it will encourage and inspire your child's creativity.

Objective 3: To develop a plan to provide long uninterrupted stretches of time and proper materials and tools for creative play.

Starting a Creative Project

Tools, time, and materials—that's what children need. With your child in mind, make a list of tools and materials they will need to pursue one of the alternative activities you envisioned in part two. We'll talk about time later.

1. Name the activity: _____.

2. Materials needed: Here's a starter list, based on our experience, that will cover most construction projects: measuring tape, pencils, magnifying glass, flat work surface with vise, hammer and nails, shovel, pliers, screwdrivers and screws, staples and stapler, glue, wheels, Styrofoam, safe drill and drill bits, electrical tape, cardboard and cardboard boxes, building

blocks, play dough, sand, wood, sandpaper, files, plastic, metal components, dust mask and safety glasses, markers, chalk, needle, thread/twine and cloth or leather, string, scissors, handsaw, jars, shelves, and an "everything drawer."

3. In terms of power tools, you'll have to decide based on your child's maturity and level of responsibility. But the basics for construction are: glue gun and sticks, electric drill, power saw, and power screwdriver (a Dremel tool can cover several of these). Materials for other projects might include: a sewing machine and a barrel of old clothes, cooking utensils and supplies, a playhouse with all its components, musical instruments, paints, canvas or paper, and easel.

The list extends beyond crafts to mechanics, sports, writing, dancing, speaking, recording, photography, videography, and collecting various things from stamps to stones to starfish. It is never ending. And it's not really a matter of cost, since the basic materials or tools needed for most of these creative projects can be purchased for less than the cost of a couple of video games or electronic gadgets that can become "boring" by the middle of Christmas day. The basic issue is discerning the ongoing script of your child's creative image, and then being willing to "go the extra mile" to nurture and develop that gift.

Discuss

Now let's talk about time. Define and discuss "long" and "uninterrupted" and how this might impact such things as the family's daily (and weekly) schedule, extracurricular activities, philosophy relating to chores, curfews, etc.

Reflection/Sharing

1. Personal: As the group discusses this question, make notes about what may have to change in order for you to implement your plan to provide creative opportunities for your child(ren).

2. Integrate these into your plan, which you should try to articulate in a sentence or two.

3. Share your plan with the group, if you wish.

Note:
Examples of creative domains include art, baking, calligraphy, canoeing, computers, conversation, cooking, dancing, decorating, design, fencing, fly-fishing, flying model airplanes, football, forestry, gardening, mechanics, music, nature studies, piano, polo, publishing, reading, sailing, skiing, teaching, tennis. There are thousands of domains that make life interesting and meaningful. Each domain has its own special rules, skills, knowledge, boundaries, and procedures.

Objective 4: To develop a plan to discover your child's creative domain(s).

For many, their creative domain starts as an interest, develops into a hobby, and then becomes an avocation that blossoms and bears fruit as a lifelong vocation. I love that word *vocation*, because it means "calling," which is the whole point I'm trying to make: *God calls each of us to fulfill some purpose in life.* His calling is consistent with the creative image of Himself in us, which is most effectively exercised within a particular creative domain.

We can help our children discover their creative domains by exposing them to a variety of arenas in which creativity is required—arenas they like and in which they may even be especially gifted. The key here is broad exposure. To specialize and focus on one area too soon may overlook the child's primary area of creativity, and may throw them out of balance.

But at some point it will be time to zero in on at least one domain. The most challenging part is keeping abreast of the changing abilities and desires of a growing child. It's like shooting at a moving target, since creativity is by nature dynamic.

Too often, we assume that some domains are off-limits—for example, mechanics or construction for girls; cooking or dancing for boys. Such assumptions have stifled and impoverished many lives. The creative urge is strong in children. Like steam in a boiling kettle, it will find a way to express itself, even in the face of withering suppression—not out of defiance, but out of deference to the One whose Spirit is empowering the child in question.

Reflection/Journaling/Discussion

Based on your observations and knowledge of your child(ren), what do you think his/her/their creative domain(s) are?

Objective 5: To formulate a plan to develop your child's creative domain(s).

Not every child is a prodigy. Unusual talents, gifts, and abilities are not prerequisites for creativity. The script God has written for each person is only revealed as it is lived. What we can do is protect and cultivate the qualities necessary for creativity, which are innate in most children—a keen curiosity about one's surroundings, awe about the mysteries of life, and an insatiable passion to solve them.

When I was in junior high, I started wood carving. My parents bought me *How to Do Wood Carving*, by John Lacey. Now, as I thumb through its yellowed pages, the old-book smell and finger smudges connect me with a wonderful boyhood memory of whittling. My parents equipped me with German-made knives and quality pieces of wood. At first I used pine, but I soon advanced to hardwoods—my favorites being walnut and maple. I still love

---

◎ Have someone read this aloud.

He has made everything beautiful in its time. Also He has put eternity in their hearts. (Ecclesiastes 3:11)

Rejoice, O young man, in your youth, and let your heart cheer you in the days of your youth; walk in the ways of your heart. (Ecclesiastes 11:9)

◎ Have someone read this aloud.

the smell of freshly sanded walnut. I carved in my bedroom, on the workbench Dad had built, taking as long as three days to make a whitetail deer. Over time my hobby produced piles of wood chips and sawdust that I tracked all over the house. Mom and Dad ignored the mess, because they knew it was temporary, and focused instead on my creations—and my creativity, which they knew would be a lifelong pursuit. Their encouragement and praises taught me to do the same for my own children, and now I smile when I find wood chips leading from all parts of the house to Dawson's bedroom.

We can easily miss this process of discovery and growth in our own child, if we are constantly distracted by matters of lesser importance—such as paying the mortgage, advancing a career, attending committee meetings, or just keeping the floors uncluttered and free from wood chips. Worse, we can put out the fire by critiquing instead of encouraging, or by dictating instead of enjoying the script.

⊚ Have someone read this aloud.

Our role as parents is to facilitate. It is God who is at work in our child "both to will and to do for His good pleasure" (Philippians 2:13). Hindering His will and work dishonors God, who has gifted our child in a particular, unique way. We must not limit our children to what we can imagine, but try to discover their passions, and then follow those passions where they lead. If we don't, they will become discouraged. If, through God's grace, they do develop a creative domain without our help, we will have forfeited the great joy of romancing them through our relationship.

When we consider our child's creative image and the domains in which it might be best expressed, we should try to see the horizons of possibilities as broadly as God sees them. Just as the body needs all its parts, so the body of Christ, of which we—adults *and* children—are members, needs all the creative gifts God has given in order to function most effectively (see 1 Corinthians 12–14). Not everyone can be a painter, poet, politician, or pastor. We all have lofty dreams for our children, but the crucial issue is not our vision, but theirs—or more important, God's vision for their creative role in His story. Mechanic or missionary (or both), it's His calling that counts.

A child needs our help to develop skills, abilities, and talents in a particular creative domain. We should provide proper equipment and seek out coaches or mentors when the child is ready. A mentor is a Christian older than our child, usually an adult, who shares one of their passions and has time to be a kindred spirit. This could be a plumber, musician, doctor, rancher, computer engineer, carpenter, or homemaker. If we can show our children someone who is "cool," who also embraces our values, principles, and beliefs, this will both draw and woo their hearts, and reinforce our training.

Sharing

Share your vision and strategy to develop your child's creative domain(s).

PREPARATION FOR COMMENCEMENT:

Be sure to read through the "commencement" session, noting all "props" that will be needed in order to complete the activities (i.e., a metal tube or clay pot, sand, and a candle that each participant brings). Establish with the group all the details of how this session will be handled—for example, an extended session, a half-day retreat; overnight retreat. Ask for volunteers to help with various details, depending on which format seems best for your group.

Note:
After this session, finalize your vision and strategy and sign the covenant toward the end of the manual. Return to this often, remembering that romancing a heart is a process, not an event, a dynamic endeavor that will grow and change as your relationship with your child does the same until, someday, you will become not parent and child, but brothers and sisters in the everlasting family of God.

FOLLOWING THROUGH AS YOUR ARROW IS RELEASED

He who binds to himself a Joy
Doth the winged life destroy;
But he who kisses the Joy as it flies
Lives in Eternity's sunrise.

WILLIAM BLAKE

Note:
This "commencement" exercise can be done as a couple in private, or as two or more couples together or in a group setting. In either case, the best setting may be a short retreat—all day Saturday, for example, or even overnight. Suggestions for a "commencement" retreat are included at the end of this section.)

◎ Have someone read this aloud.

The climax of the romance is the release. Releasing an arrow or a child is not an event, but a process involving a series of events. It is both enchanting and terrifying to let go. In archery, this series of events happens in the blink of an eye. In parenting, the process is much longer, although in retrospect it may seem but the blink of an eye. I tried to capture this lyrically in the song "Arrows":

And time seems to fly,
Oh the years pass so quickly now,
Like sand through your fingers
You hold it once and then it's gone.

The children keep changing
They grow as the years rush by
Like arrows in a quiver
They're made to someday fly.

Share

1. What is (or will be) your greatest concern when it is time to release your child into the world?

2. How can your friends (including participants in the group) support you?

LEADER'S PRAYER: *Father, we now have a vision and a strategy for winning the hearts of our children. We are excited, but also nervous and anxious. We know all too well that our best efforts will be fraught with flaws. Father, please fill in the gaps and shine through them as well. We need discernment to see the best way to romance their hearts, wisdom to know how, and courage to follow through. We ask for these things. We also acknowledge that we need to support and be supported by our fellow pilgrims in this process, so we ask that You would show us, perhaps through what we're about to hear and experience, how to best accomplish this. In Jesus' name, amen.*

SESSION GOAL: To encourage participants to follow through in their parenting by entrusting their children to God, in whose hands our "arrows" become His "winsome warriors" to win the world to Himself.

SESSION OBJECTIVES

1. To see how investing faith in our children is the most effective parenting strategy as they leave.

2. To understand that the final act of romancing our children's hearts is to release them with confidence to the Original Romancer, who has a purpose for them, perhaps beyond what we might dare to ask or think.

◎ Have someone read this aloud.

A friend of mine was discipling a college student who had dabbled in drugs and had run around with the wrong crowd, but whose heart now desired God. My friend asked him, "Why did you come back to God?" The young man said, "When I was in high school, every morning my father drove me to school. And as I opened the car door he never failed to reach over, put his hand on my arm, and say, 'Son, remember, I believe in you.' This one statement, more than anything else, kept me from getting into serious trouble. It has wooed me back to God. Those words haunted me as I strayed. They reached something deep inside me and called me to be better. I have finally begun living up to the faith my dad had in me. He saw something in me I didn't see—his son conformed to the image of Christ. He romanced me to this image."

The way this father saw his son is parallel to the way God views all who trust in Christ for salvation—as already made perfect through His grace. The Greek root for *belief* simply means to "give one's heart to." This is how perfect love casts out fear—and the need to prove anything. The question for the child—whether in physical or spiritual terms—becomes: "How can I honor someone who has such faith in me?"

But what if a child has not earned our trust, or has squandered it in the past? Trust may be conditional, but faith is not. The father believed in his son who was a prodigal. This is risky, but it is also where grace comes in. A parent who has faith in a child who seems unworthy of trust may be surprised by the response, as children tend to live up (or down) to the image we see in them. Of course there are no guarantees where humans are concerned, but grace-filled love woos the heart, while love that "keeps books" only pushes its object further away.

Although children are gifts from God, and a believer with a full quiver is blessed, many Christian parents are too concerned with what the neighbors, their larger family, or church members will think of them if their children seem to be crooked arrows. Real love—the kind that God expressed for us through Jesus—is risky and sometimes very costly.

Jesus gave His life for undeserving, wayward sinners—including us and our children—because He believed that the will of His Father was good, and that His Word was trustworthy.

Reflection/Discussion

1. Do you think that children tend to live up (or down) to the image we see in them?

2. Imagine for a moment what your children perceive to be your expectations of them:

    __ That they will make some great contribution to the human race.
    __ That they will be good people.
    __ That they'll be the athlete/dancer/musician I never was.
    __ That they'll become rich and famous.
    __ That they'll become professionals, such as doctors, lawyers, ministers, professors, or scientists.
    __ That they'll become spiritual "giants"—missionaries, theologians, or evangelists.
    __ Other: _____.

3. In a sentence, describe what you think are God's expectations of your child. Share your answer.

◎ Have someone read
this aloud.

*Like arrows in the hand of a
warrior, so are the children
of one's youth. [Blessed] is
the man who has his quiver
full of them. (Psalms 127:4)*

◎ Read introduction,
then discuss.

*Therefore encourage one
another and build each
other up, just as in fact
you are doing.
(1 Thessalonians 5:11, NIV)*

Psalm 127:4 usually brings to mind the comforting vision of a parent enjoying the pleasures of a full quiver of children and the security they provide in old age. But the context is war—the spiritual conflict of the ages being waged even as you read. The quiver belongs to a warrior whose desire is to obtain as many arrows as possible to shoot into, through, and even behind enemy lines.

To imagine our precious children involved in a direct D day–style spiritual attack, penetrating Satan's stronghold, is startling. To envision them as special forces infiltrating the most dangerous territory of all is almost too much to bear.

Psalm 127:4 and Ephesians 5:1 imply that our children are to be winsome warriors among the enemy, and sometimes they fly so high and far that we will be uncomfortable and thrilled at the same time. Personally, I never bargained for this much drama. But this is the purpose of parenting. Romancing our child's heart is all about lifting our sights above our human vision, to the context of the Larger Story.

For all of us as parents, the moment when our children are ready to be released comes much sooner than we think. But the quiver is God's, and on His bow they will fly according to His good purpose and pleasure.

During these past three months you've weighed many ideas and discussed many questions related to embracing a vision and crafting a parenting strategy to win your child's heart. Review the most significant of these now as you prepare to share the personal vision and strategy that have emerged.

1. Looking back over the entire experience, including reading the book, working through the manual, and participating in the group, share what is most vivid—an insight, experience, observation, etc.

2. As a result of this process, what changes (or refinements) have you made (or do you plan to make) in your parenting. Or what convictions about parenting have been reinforced?

Covenanting Together

Sitting in a circle, each person or each couple lights a candle and then shares part or all of their personal vision and strategy for winning their child's heart. Each then reads their covenant, asking group members to be their witnesses.

After each person or couple shares their vision, strategy, and covenant, their "witnesses" will pray that the Holy Spirit of God will guide and empower the person or couple to fulfill the desire of their heart(s).

After they share their vision and strategy, they place their burning candles in sand in a metal tub or clay pot in the middle of the circle of participants. By the end all the candles will start melting/falling together toward the center, symbolizing the special union/communion that the group has experienced.

Finish with a song, or with a general prayer of dedication or blessing.

RETREAT IDEAS

1. Your goal is to have an experience of fellowship, dedication, and covenant. Suggestions for a half-day retreat include: morning with a lunch together, afternoon with a dinner together in a home, at church, at a retreat center, a camping trip, a motel with a meeting room/suite, bed-and-breakfast, anywhere that will allow for uninterrupted sharing.

2. Suggestions for meal(s): If various group members are cooks and want to contribute to a smorgasbord, then someone should coordinate the effort. The one thing to avoid is for anyone to get so involved with meal preparation that he or she, like Martha (sister of Lazarus), becomes anxious about this rather than using the time leading up to the retreat to be prepared to participate in the spiritual smorgasbord.

3. If the retreat is longer than a half day, music and film clips might help establish an atmosphere conducive to accomplishing the event's purpose. Someone who plays guitar could be assigned to lead some worship. Film clips could focus on themes from the study just completed; for example, one might capture that inspirational moment when someone or a team is entering a competition or even a critical time in a romance when the person is not sure of the outcome but is plunging in, nonetheless. These clips could communicate the emotions of this retreat—parents engaging in the contest for their child's heart.

PERSONAL STRATEGY WORKSHEETS

My strategy for winning my child's heart:

Identify your vision/goal—the big picture you would like to see for each of your children.

Vision/Goal

_____

_____

_____

_____

_____

_____

_____

_____

_____

_____

_____

_____

_____

_____

_____

_____

Study   Gather ideas, knowledge, and insights relevant to that goal—from your own experience, this parenting group/class, and personal research or study.

_____

_____

_____

_____

_____

_____

_____

_____

_____

Objectives   Identify tactical steps that lead toward fulfilling the vision and accomplishing your goal for each of your children.

_____

_____

_____

_____

_____

_____

_____

_____

_____

_____

Develop a logical and practical plan for fulfilling the vision and accomplishing your goal(s). [Note: A calendar will be one of your most important tools, for linking specific dates with your goals. It will both motivate and document your progress.]

Rationale

_____

_____

_____

_____

_____

_____

_____

_____

_____

Put your plan into practice.

Act

_____

_____

_____

_____

_____

_____

_____

_____

_____

PERSONAL COVENANT

Before God, and with the help of His Spirit, I hereby acknowledge that, as a Christian, my desire is to love God with my heart, soul, mind, and strength. I further acknowledge that as a Christian parent, my highest calling is to win [_____] to
child's name
Christ, who is my vision.

I will seek to fulfill this calling in the same way He won my heart—through incarnational romance—knowing full well that entering [_____]'s world for
child's name
this purpose will require sacrifice of me, including my time, energy, and money, but most of all my parental power, which I acknowledge is powerless when it comes to matters of the heart.

I will prepare for this privilege by fulfilling the prerequisites to romance, after which I will strive to develop the characteristics and wield the tools of a romancer. I will protect and cultivate [_____]'s sense of wonder by so intimately immersing
child's name
[_____] in the creation that [_____] longs to know
child's name   child's name
its Creator. I will also protect and cultivate the creative image of God in [_____]
child's name
and do everything in my power to help [_____] discover and develop the
child's name
creative domains(s) in which this creative image is expressed.

When the time has come, I will release [_____] with faith, hope, and
child's name
joy…an "arrow" that will fly not only straight and true, but high and far, winning other hearts for Jesus as theirs have been won, with the sacred romance of God's love.

This "covenant" is intended as an example of what yours may look like when it is done. Feel free to use/not use any or all of it.

Signed: _____   Date: _____

Signed: _____   Date: _____

Witness: _____   Witness: _____

NOTES

1. Eleanor H. Porter, *Pollyanna* (Boston: L.C. Pages & Co., 1913 edition), 42–5.

2. Karey Swan, *Hearth and Home* (Sisters, OR: Loyal Publishing, 2002), 188, 191.

3. Adapted by the authors from the parable by Danish philosopher/theologian Søren Kierkegaard, in *Philosophical Fragments,* 31–43, cited by Philip Yancey in *Disappointment with God,* 103–4.

4. Richard J. Foster, *Streams of Living Water* (San Francisco: HarperSanFrancisco, 1998).

JOURNAL

_____

_____

_____

_____

_____

_____

_____

_____

_____

_____

_____

_____

_____

_____

_____

_____

_____

_____